An Introduction to the Philosophy of Religion

Introducing Philosophy

Introducing Philosophy is a series of textbooks designed to introduce the basic topics of philosophy for any student approaching the subject for the first time. Each volume presents a central subject of philosophy by considering the key issues and outlooks associated with the area. With the emphasis firmly on the arguments for and against a philosophical position, the reader is encouraged to think philosophically about the subject.

1 An Introduction to the Philosophy of Religion
B. R. Tilghman

An Introduction to the Philosophy of Religion

B. R. Tilghman

BLACKWELL
Oxford UK & Cambridge USA

First published 1994

Blackwell Publishers
238 Main Street
Cambridge, Massachusetts 02142
USA

108 Cowley Road
Oxford OX4 1JF
UK

Library of Congress Cataloging-in-Publication Data

Tilghman, Benjamin R.
An introduction to the philosophy of religion / B. R. Tilghman.
p. cm. – (Introducing philosophy)
Includes bibliographical references and index.
ISBN 0-631-18937-8. – ISBN 0-631-18938-6 (pbk.)
1. Religion – Philosophy. I. Title. II. Series.
BL 51.T55 1994
210–dc20 93-25753
CIP

British Library Cataloguing in Publication Data

A CIP catalogue record for this book is available from the British Library.

Typeset in 11½ on 13½pt Bembo
by Photoprint, Torquay, Devon
Printed in the USA

This book is printed on acid-free paper.

Contents

Preface Addressed to the Instructor

This book is intended primarily for undergraduate students with no previous study of philosophy, but other people are also welcome to read it. The book differs from the usual introductory textbooks in the philosophy of religion in several respects. It makes no attempt at being a survey of the principal problems and questions in the field or at providing a catalogue of the possible positions that can be taken with respect to those questions. It does, however, examine several issues that I have found to be of interest to students: the existence of God, the truth of the Bible, the relation between religion and science, and the relation between religion and ethics. I have sought to present these topics as something other than abstract intellectual exercises. In each case I have tried to place the topics and the philosophers who discuss them in an historical and intellectual context and to show how that context influenced the way the questions were treated. Then I have tried to show how these topics and issues make contact with the actual religious beliefs and practices of people now and the problems they raise for contemporary religious life.

It also differs by starting with the origins of philosophy among the Greeks and the development of the conception of God that both Judaism and Christianity have inherited from the ancient Israelites. A good bit of attention is paid to the nature of argument, to logic, to method in both science and scholarship, and, of course, to philosophical method. The book proceeds from a particular view about the nature of philosophy and its problems; it advances theses about the various questions and problems encountered on the way and even advances a modest thesis about the nature of religious life and belief. I have tried to present these theses as suggestions for resolving the questions rather than asserting flatly that this is how things are. By reading them this way students may be more inclined to try them, discuss them, and in some cases discard them. In the examination of the various issues I do not, however, scruple to call a bad argument a bad argument and I make no apologies for that.

The six chapters of the book are intended to display a certain organization and contribute to an ultimate conclusion. The first chapter sketches the development of science and philosophy in ancient Greece and the monotheistic conception of God in ancient Israel and later Judaism and indicates how the philosophy of religion arose in the Christian melding of Judaic religious beliefs with Greek philosophy. Chapter 2 reviews some of the traditional proofs for the existence of God and finds them all unsuccessful despite their containing some material of genuine religious importance. Chapter 3 considers the truth of the Bible. The doctrine of Biblical inerrancy is explained and then contrasted with the results of serious modern Biblical scholarship. The fourth chapter discusses the historical relation between religion and science and recent controversies over such things as Creationism. Chapter 5 is concerned with religion and ethics and discusses the logic of theological ethics and the traditional problem of evil. The final chapter ties up a number of loose ends accumulated in the earlier chapters. The arguments for the existence of God won't work; the Bible cannot be considered an historical record of God's activity in the world; science cannot give support to religious beliefs. In the light of these obstacles to certain traditional ways of understanding religion, what becomes of religion? One modern response is to dismiss the business as outmoded nonsense. I do offer suggestions about how religious life and belief may be understood when it is stripped of the hindrance of shabby intellectual baggage.

Philosophy is a different sort of beast from many other disciplines. In the sciences and mathematics, for example, things are pretty well established and there is virtually no disagreement about the material at the elementary level (what goes on at the frontiers of those disciplines is another matter). What is wanted in those areas are textbooks that present this material clearly and in a well-ordered fashion. By contrast there is not all that much agreement about exactly what the nature of philosophy is and what the content of an introductory course should be. The questions of philosophy seem to recur perennially and those questions and the philosophers who espouse them are subject to perennial rethinking and reevaluating. Let us not, however, suppose that this entails that there are no intellectual standards or that one can say just anything about a philosophical question without fear of being taken to task.

The undergraduate study of philosophy has to have some special value that sets it apart from the teaching that is done in many other disciplines. It has to be more than merely intellectual or cultural history or survey of the Great Books. It must, in fact, do several things. It must train students to read a serious work closely and carefully with several questions in mind: (1) What is the problem or question that the author is addressing and why is it a problem? How does the issue arise out of our own concerns for the subject? Students should be encouraged to make the problem their own and to be drawn into the puzzlement that leads us to do philosophy. (2) What is the author's strategy for solving that problem or answering that question? (3) What is the conclusion reached that is supposed to solve the problem or answer the question? How is that conclusion argued for? Unlike the results of many other disciplines, the conclusions of philosophers are unintelligible apart from the arguments that got them there. (4) Are the conclusions true or otherwise satisfactory? Do they even make sense? (5) Has the question that got the whole thing started perhaps been misconceived? And, if so, do we need to back up and start all over again? Any undergraduate course that can do these things will be successful. There is, needless to say, much more for the study of philosophy to do, but that will have to come later.

It is of the greatest importance that students be taught to separate the intellectual wheat from the intellectual chaff, the true from the false, sense from nonsense, and what is worthwhile from the shoddy. All this contributes to why I do not choose to present a philosophical position and then list the arguments in favor of the position and the arguments against it, leaving, in effect, readers to pay their money and take their choice. If one does not have some views about the right way to go in philosophy, then one has no business teaching it. If you object to my way of describing and dealing with some issue, why, then you have something to argue against.

If the focus of an undergraduate course is to be on reading original works, then why a text book? In a number of cases one does want to ask, "Why, indeed?" In teaching a philosophy course I much prefer to read the philosophers and make my own mistakes in understanding them than not to read them and rely on the mistakes of the author of an expository textbook. This book is not intended to be a substitute for reading St Anselm, St Thomas, David Hume, and the others. It is intended, rather, to be a help and a guide in reading them and in digging out the problems. It should be used alongside the original texts. More than likely it contains mistakes and assuredly there are things that other philosophers will disagree with. That is not at all bad. Calling attention to mistakes is sometimes one of the best ways to bring to light the correct view and properly focused disagreements can help to sharpen the understanding of the problem. If the book succeeds in doing that, it will have served one of its purposes.

Religion is one of the most important aspects of human life; indeed, for many people it is the most important aspect. Its importance does not have to be argued for nor should it appear as an *assumption* of the book, as if there could be other assumptions about it. What we must constantly be reminded of, however, especially when we are doing philosophy, is that religion is a part of *life* and is not merely a set of beliefs, doctrines, or propositions that can be held or rejected or debated in abstraction from that life.

This intimate connection of religion with life makes the philosophy of religion one of the most exciting undergraduate courses to teach. Students come to the course with the kind of vital interest in the subject that they rarely muster for philosophical staples such as epistemology and metaphysics. Many who are religious want to see their beliefs defended and justified; those who are opposed to religion want to see the whole thing exposed as fraud. Very few are neutral. The challenge to the instructor is to keep this vitality within the proper intellectual channels. Statements of personal belief and "testimony" must be declared out of order from the beginning. The students must be made to come to grips with the particulars of the text and with the details of the arguments. They cannot be permitted to ignore an argument because they find it uncongenial. Any instructor who is able to get students to take arguments seriously and to face problems honestly will be successful.

The book is an articulation and systemization of material that I have been teaching in introductory courses in the philosophy of religion for a number of years. This material has at times been very well received by students. I do not know how other instructors will receive it; I can only hope that it will be of help to them and to their students.

Introduction

This is a book about the philosophy of religion. It is intended for students and anyone else who is interested in the topic, but who does not know anything about philosophy. Thus I will do my best not to presuppose any knowledge of philosophy as we go along and to explain things as we get to them. If you have already studied or read some philosophy you may find yourself being led over some familiar ground, but a second tour of the landscape can surely do no harm and may even lead to seeing some of the sights missed on the first go round or seeing them from a different angle.

It is common for an introductory study to begin with a definition or general characterization of its subject matter so it is only reasonable that you want to know what this thing called the philosophy of religion is. It seems obvious that to understand what the philosophy of religion is we will have to understand something of both religion and philosophy. While most of us have more or less some idea of what religion is, few of us have any clear idea at all of what philosophy is. It is not the idea of religion that troubles us at the outset – although it may trouble us later on – but the idea of philosophy. The word "philosophy" was coined in the fifth century BC from two Greek words, *philos*, which means "love," and *sophia*, which means "wisdom." So philosophy is the love of wisdom and a philosopher is a lover of wisdom. While this is an interesting historical fact about the word, it really doesn't tell us very much because we still have to find out what is meant by wisdom and what it means to love it. Etymology aside, there is no want of definitions of philosophy, but they tend to be inaccurate, obfuscating, or intelligible only to someone who already had some competence in philosophy. These definitions and descriptions run from the pretentious:

> [Philosophy's] object is to take over the results of the various sciences, to add to them the results of the religious and ethical experiences of mankind, and then to reflect upon the whole. The hope is that, by this means, we may be able to reach some general conclusions as to the nature of the Universe, and as to our position and prospects in it.[1]

to the enigmatic: the aim of philosophy is to show the fly the way out of the fly bottle;[2] to the just plain silly: the goal of philosophy is said to be "*Autonomy*: the freedom of being able to decide for yourself what you will believe by using your own reasoning abilities."[3]

The word "philosophy" has been used in many different ways. Over the centuries it has referred to a variety of activities. At one time or another almost any kind of scientific or intellectual activity got called philosophy, including even magic and the occult. Isaac Newton called his great work which is the foundation of modern mechanics *Mathematical Principles of Natural Philosophy*. The natural sciences of physics, chemistry, and biology were still often referred to as natural philosophy until well into the nineteenth century.

It is common to speak of a person's philosophy of life. What is usually meant here is some general attitude toward the world and other people. One person, for example, may be an optimist and always tends to look on the bright side of things while another tends to be cynical in his or her relations to and estimation of others. Too often these "philosophies" are expressed in banal formulas such as the optimist's "Face the sun and the shadows fall behind you" or the cynic's "Do unto others before they do unto you." This sort of thing can give philosophy a bad name.

Politicians standing for office may refer to their party's philosophy of a fair deal for the little man and a company can boast of its philosophy of seeking to provide the best services at the lowest possible price. In this use of the word, "philosophy" is really a synonym for "policy." Since we have the perfectly good English word "policy" for such things, it should be used when that is what is meant. There is no point in putting an undue strain on the other word; our language is under enough stress as it is these days.

In the twentieth century philosophy has become an independent discipline within the academic organization of universities. Academic philosophers think of themselves as professionals and intensive postgraduate studies are designed for the training of professional philosophers. Even among professional philosophers, however, there is little agreement about exactly what philosophy is and what it is trying to do. Philosophers in Britain and the United States, for example, by and large have thought about and practiced their trade of philosophy rather differently from the way their colleagues have in France and Germany.

We shall not begin with a definition or even a broad characterization of the philosophy of religion, much less of philosophy in general. We shall not even begin with a definition of religion. The word "philosophy" has been used to cover too many activities and there is too much disagreement about exactly what it is for it to be summed up in any neat formula. This does not mean, however, that philosophy can be just anything you want it to be. To be frank, this book is written with a particular conception of philosophy and its problems and methods in mind. But we won't even want to begin with a general characterization of that conception of philosophy. That is not because it is esoteric or highly technical, but simply because no account of it could possibly mean anything to people who have not already got their feet wet, as it were, in philosophical waters. It is something that must be made clear by means of various examples and the commentary that goes along with them. Something about what philosophy is and what makes a problem a philosophical one will emerge little by little as we go along.

Although nothing is served at this point by trying to define philosophy in general or the philosophy of religion in particular, we can, nevertheless, say something about what philosophy as we understand it is not. It is not a philosophy of life in the sense of some general attitude or orientation to life, the world, and other people. It is not the policies we adopt for this or that project or purpose. With respect to the philosophy of religion we can say that, whatever the philosophy of religion is, it is not religious instruction. It is not the aim of the philosophy of religion to make anyone religious; the philosopher's job is not to instruct an audience in doctrine or to teach anyone to pray, observe forms of worship or generally encourage piety. If that is to be done, it is to be done in the churches, synagogues, and even the family. And it is certainly not the aim of philosophy to show that the beliefs of religion are reasonable and true and that it becomes rational people to be religious nor to show that religion is really only outmoded superstition. It is not philosophy's job to make a case either for or against religion.

Nor must the philosophy of religion be confused with the academic discipline called comparative religion. Comparative religion is the study and comparison of the beliefs and practices of the many different religions found around the world, Judaism, Christianity, Islam, Hinduism, Buddhism, Taoism, Shinto, the religions of the so-called primitive societies of Africa and the Pacific islands, and so on and on. While philosophers may occasionally make use of the information provided by comparative religion, their job is not to describe and compare.

The conclusions of philosophy do not form a body of knowledge or store of information about a particular subject matter. In this respect philosophy is rather different from the various sciences and fields such as history, sociology, or anthropology. Philosophy can be described as an activity, but what kind of an activity it is must be shown as we go along.

Since it is intended as an introduction, this book presupposes no knowledge of philosophy although it does presuppose some knowledge of religion. This is because the philosophy of religion requires us to work with questions and issues that arise when we think, puzzle, and reflect about religious beliefs and religious practices. If we don't know anything at all about religion, then we cannot begin to understand what these issues are or why they should be important to anyone and religion is obviously a very important aspect of people's lives. This circumstance is not unique to the philosophy of religion. The issues that philosophers study can arise out of almost any area of human thought and activity and it is from within those areas that the philosophical questions are generated. An obvious example of this is ethics or, as it used to be called, moral philosophy, that part of philosophy in which we think about the nature of the moral aspects of our lives. It is equally true of the philosophy of science and the philosophy of mathematics.

To study ethics we need no specialized knowledge of any particular branch of human practice. We need only some experience in life, some experience in which we make judgments and decisions about the rightness and wrongness of actions and in which we find people and situations good or bad. This kind of experience is common to all of us except children below the age of reason, the feeble-minded and perhaps the sociopath. It is not like that, of course, with the philosophy of science or the philosophy of mathematics where at least an educated acquaintance with science and mathematics is necessary although one need not be either a scientist or a mathematician to get involved in either branch of philosophy. By contrast with ethics, however, most people do not have even an educated acquaintance with these fields.

How is it with the philosophy of religion? I said that *some* knowledge of religion is necessary. This does not entail that in order to understand the philosophy of religion you have to be religious, that is, that you have to have religious faith or be a churchgoer or anything of the sort. You must, however, know something about what the religious beliefs and doctrines are that people profess and what the practices and forms of worship are that people engage in. With respect to religion we may make a very rough classification of people into three groups. There are those who can be described as religious; there are those who are indifferent to religion; and then there are others such as militant atheists who are downright hostile to religion. It is clear, I think, that even these latter two groups know something about these things, if not from their own lives within the religious context of family, church, or synagogue, at least from the observation of the religious lives of their neighbors.

Our study in this book has two limitations that ought to be acknowledged right from the beginning. We shall make no attempt to survey *all* the problems of the philosophy of religion – as if there might be a definitive roster of those problems – but only examine a few of those problems. Nor will we attempt to review all the various positions that have been taken with respect to those problems. Secondly we will confine ourselves only to questions that arise out of the major monotheistic religions of Judaism, Christianity, and Islam with the emphasis on the first two. There are more than enough issues here to keep us busy without taking on additional burdens.

It is this latter limitation that ensures that we have at least the minimal acquaintance with religion that is necessary to get the philosophical questions going. That western civilization and its traditions are in large measure the product of a Judeo-Christian heritage is a commonplace, nevertheless it is a commonplace that must be kept in mind. The influence of this heritage surrounds us and cannot be avoided even when we do not think of ourselves as religious or even explicitly reject a religious affiliation.[4]

Before quitting these introductory remarks and getting on to the real business of the philosophy of religion it may be in order to make a further comment or two about philosophy. Although I have not said what philosophy is I did comment in passing that philosophy is now a professional academic discipline. The student or the layman or casual reader of this book should not be daunted or cowed by that fact. Philosophers are not necessarily people others should stand in awe of. Awe is a serious business and should be reserved for proper objects. I mentioned earlier that philosophy is an activity and you are invited to join in this activity. The practice of philosophy, however, will make demands upon you; it will demand that you read closely and think carefully, that you articulate your thoughts clearly and that you be willing to see your own ideas laid out upon the table for rational and critical scrutiny.

These demands can be especially trying when the philosophy is the philosophy of religion. For many people religion is the very center of their lives and its doctrines and practices are accepted unquestioningly. The very idea of examining these views can seem an attack upon them if not a sacrilege. It is sometimes necessary to make a special effort to disengage your religious (or anti-religious) passions and fervor, to put them out of gear, as it were, and look at the issues in what some would describe as the cold, hard light of reason. Our aim, after all, is neither to defend religion nor to attack it, but to understand certain aspects of it.

Notes

1 C. D. Broad, *Scientific Thought* (Paterson, NJ: Littlefield, Adams & Co., 1959), p. 20.
2 Ludwig Wittgenstein, *Philosophical Investigations*, 2nd edn (New York: Macmillan, 1958), §309.
3 Manuel Velasquez, *Philosophy* (Belmont, Calif.: Wadsworth Pub. Co., 1991), pp. 3–4.
4 Increasingly Islamic and Asian cultural and religious influences are making themselves felt in Europe, Britain,

and North America. My self-imposed restriction should in no way be construed as a denigration of these or any other cultural and religious traditions. One has to limit oneself one way or another and questions arising out of the Judeo-Christian tradition are simply the ones I have been concerned with.

1

Philosophy and Religion: Tracing Our Origins

The Greeks, Science, and Philosophy

The western tradition in philosophy is a product of ancient Greece while the western religious tradition of Judaism and Christianity has its origins in ancient Israel. In this chapter we will trace these two developments and come to some understanding of the intellectual and spiritual visions that made the worlds of the Greeks and the ancient Israelites as well as the later Jews so different from one another.

The beginnings of philosophy can be traced as far back as the first quarter of the sixth century BC. In the Greek world philosophy and science got started together and very early on the two were really indistinguishable. The Greeks were the only people in the ancient world to develop science and philosophy and it is natural to ask why this is so and what was unique in this development.[1]

Why it was the Greeks and not some other ancient people who invented science and philosophy is a question

body moves in just this path by reference to its mass, initial velocity, and the forces acting on it.

When people speak of theories as speculations about the facts that haven't yet been checked out they are putting theory and fact on what we may call the same logical level. A fact can be reported in a single statement. The fact that it is raining can be reported simply by saying "It is raining." We may think that we can do the same for a theory and that mention of the atomic theory, for example, amounts to saying something like "Objects in the world are made up of very little things that nobody can see" in the same way that we can say "Houses are made up of bricks and mortar." This way of speaking shows how theory and fact can seem to be on the same logical level.

From within that way of thinking there is, nevertheless, an important difference of another sort between fact and theory. If one thinks like that, then when it comes to something like atomic theory the next move consists in saying "But of course that's *just* a theory." The emphasis on the word "just" makes it clear that this is considered to be a speculation of little value that does not measure up to what we know to be solid fact.[2]

As a matter of fact, theory and fact are on quite different logical levels. A scientific theory is not a single statement about what the facts are imagined to be. Typically, a scientific theory is constructed of several technical terms and expressions together with a number of laws and principles in which these terms and expressions occur. Here it will help us to understand something about what a theory is to examine actual examples of theories developed by the Greeks. The Greeks achieved remarkable results in both geometry and astronomy and we shall look at each in turn.

"Geometry" is from the Greek and means something like "measure of the earth." This derivation suggests that geometry more than likely arose out of practical surveying needs. For practical surveying it is very useful to be able to lay out right angles. The ancient Egyptians apparently had a rule-of-thumb method for doing this and we can imagine them putting it to use in staking out the foundations for a new pyramid or laying out the goal lines for a game of Mummy Ball. They likely did it this way. In a loop of rope of sufficient length tie twelve knots at regular intervals. Put the loop around three stakes to form a triangle so that the first and second stake are separated by four intervals, the second and third stakes by three intervals and the third and the first stakes by five intervals. The angle whose corner is at stake two is a right angle (figure 1.1). Thus the Egyptians knew in a rough-and-

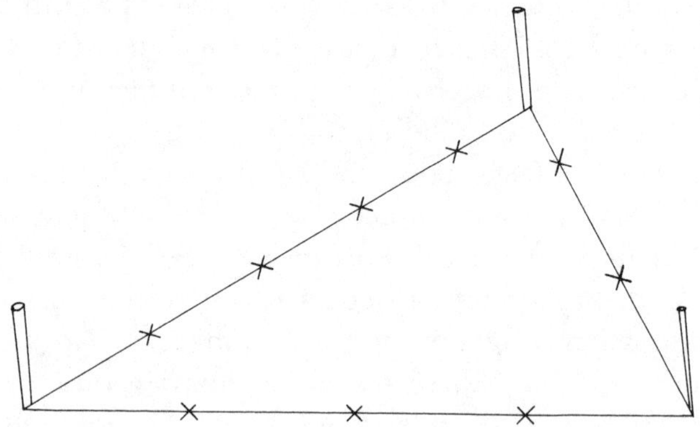

Figure 1.1

ready way that a triangle with sides measuring three, four, and five units was a right triangle.

It was part of the Greek genius not to be satisfied with the mere fact that a 3:4:5 triangle yielded a right angle. It is traditional to assign the next step to the Greek philosopher and mathematician Pythagoras, a rather shadowy figure who was active in the last half of the sixth century BC. Pythagoras is credited with the discovery that for every right triangle the square of the hypotenuse equals the sum of the squares of the other two sides. At any rate, tradition has given his name to this proposition: the Pythagorean Theorem. In our modern way of putting it, we can say that for any right triangle whose sides are a, b, and c, $a^2 + b^2 = c^2$ (figure 1.2). Thus the Greeks generalized the

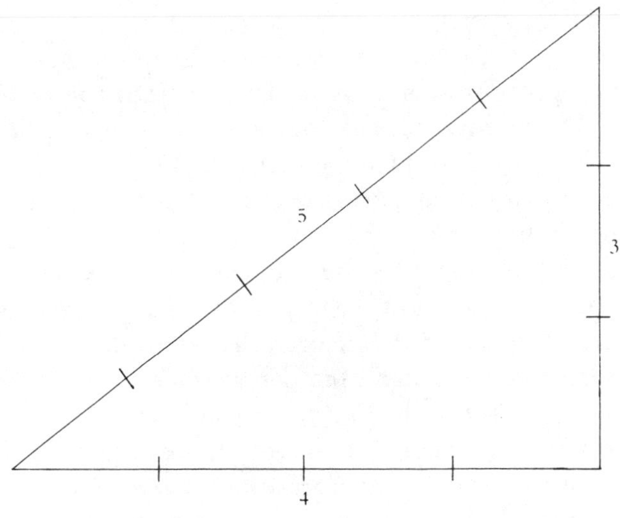

Figure 1.2

Egyptian statement. The Pythagorean formula holds for *every* right triangle; the triangle whose sides are in the proportion 3:4:5 is only one special case of the general rule.

We do not know how Pythagoras, if indeed it was he, arrived at his proposition. A sure enough proof of it, however, was provided by Euclid, a Greek living in Alexandria in Egypt who was active around 300 BC. Euclid's name is almost synonymous with geometry and his book, the *Elements*, became the basis of every school text until well into the twentieth century. Euclid's *Elements* summed up, completed, and systematized some 250 years of Greek work in geometry.[3] Euclid's great accomplishment was in this systematization. He began with a number of definitions of key notions and then provided a set of propositions about these notions that were assumed to be self-evidently true. From these statements, called axioms and postulates, he could then derive by logical deduction any number of additional propositions. The additional propositions that are derived from the axioms are called theorems and the logical derivation is called a proof. This process of proving theorems by deriving them from the axioms and postulates is familiar to everyone from high school geometry.

From within Euclid's system of geometry Pythagoras' proposition about right triangles can be proven as a theorem. The truth of the theorem had become evident to all the Greek scientists and mathematicians since the time of Pythagoras, but in the light of Euclid's work it became clear for the first time *why* it is true. If we accept Euclid's axioms and postulates, as presumably we must,[4] we understand that the theorem is a necessary logical consequence of them. And not only do we understand why it is true, but we can now see its systematic connection with all the other propositions of geometry since they are all derived from the same group of axioms.

Greek geometry was a remarkable intellectual achievement. It became an ideal or model of what a theory was supposed to be. Ideally, we could say that theory should be completely general in that it should be about *all* phenomena or facts of a certain sort, it should explain these facts, and it should make clear the interconnections between them.[5] Euclid's geometry was precisely this sort of thing. Its propositions were completely general, that is, they were about *all* straight lines, *all* planes, *all* right triangles, and so on. It provided logical explanations for why the facts of geometry are like they are and it demonstrated the systematic connections and interrelations between a vast number of geometrical facts.

Now to our second example of Greek theoretical work, i.e. astronomy. The Babylonians had been observing the heavens, stargazing we might say, since early in the second millennium BC. Over the centuries they compiled detailed records and tables of the positions and movements of the stars and planets in the heavens. From these records they were able to tell where a particular body was to be seen in the sky on any night of the year. They even had some success in predicting when eclipses of the sun and moon would occur. All this astronomical knowledge had a certain practical application in determining the turn of the seasons which was important for agriculture, and we should not fail to mention its use in astrology which was believed essential in directing human affairs.[6]

The Babylonians had collected and catalogued an enormous number of facts about the movements of the heavenly bodies, but they offered no explanations of the nature of these bodies nor why they moved as they did. In other words, they had no theory of astronomy. It was the

Greeks who began to seek theoretical explanations to make sense of all these facts.

Greek astronomical theory assumed that the earth is the center of the world and does not move, while the heavenly bodies move around the earth in circular paths. It may be difficult for us today to regard this belief as anything but an ignorant mistake; after all, everyone knows that the apparent movement of the sun across the sky is really the result of the earth turning upon its own axis. The belief, however, was not a foolish one. Have you ever seen the earth rotate? Stick your head out the window and look at the ground. It's not going anywhere. The sun you see rise every day in the east and move across the sky to set in the west.[7] Our common experience speaks in favor of the geocentric astonomy.

The assumption that heavenly motion is circular may have had something to do with the then common religious view that the heavenly bodies were gods, or, if not themselves gods, at least closely connected with the divine. Add to this the curious geometrical assumption that the circle is somehow the perfect figure and we have to understand that if there is to be divine motion it must, then, be perfect motion, that is, circular motion. So there you may have it.

It is an interesting fact about the heavenly bodies that what are called the fixed stars do not seem to change their positions relative to one another in the sky. That is why they are called the fixed stars. The stars do, however, move about the sky every night, but they all move together. They move as if they are all turning about the pole star. Imagine that the stars are all attached to a sphere which turns upon an axis. Imagine this axis running through the poles of the earth right up to the pole star. The rotation of this sphere about its axis every twenty-four hours explains very tidily the observed motion of the stars.

This explanation, however, will not do for the motion of the sun, the moon, and the planets. These bodies do not move along with the fixed stars, but vary their positions against the background of the stars. This variation was particularly vexing in the case of the planets. A planet will be seen to move from east to west across the background of the stars for some nights and then stop and move backwards for a period before starting its westward motion again. Its path looked like that shown in figure 1.3. It was this curious motion that led to the planets being called "planets" for the word in Greek means "wanderer." The problem for the Greek astronomers was how to explain the motion of the planets in terms of the theoretical assumption that all heavenly motion is circular.

The final solution to this problem was worked out by another Alexandrian Greek named Claudius Ptolemy in the middle of the second century AD. Like Euclid before

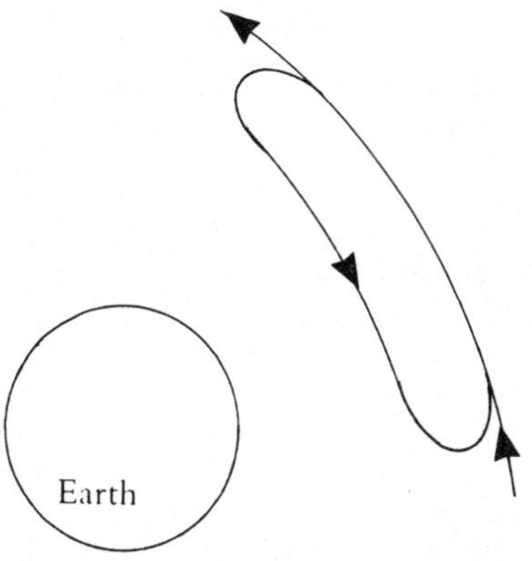

Figure 1.3

him with geometry, Ptolemy summed up and completed the astronomical work that the Greeks had begun seven centuries before. The astronomer wants to imagine the planet moving on a circle or sphere centered on the earth, but the planet does not exhibit the kind of uniform motion that would represent. Imagine a smaller circle called an epicycle centered on the original circle. This smaller circle has two motions. It revolves around that center and that center then moves around the larger circle. If the planet is assumed to be attached to the epicycle its motion will trace a curve like that shown in figure 1.4.

Thus at certain points in its orbit the planet will appear to be moving forward in the sky and at certain

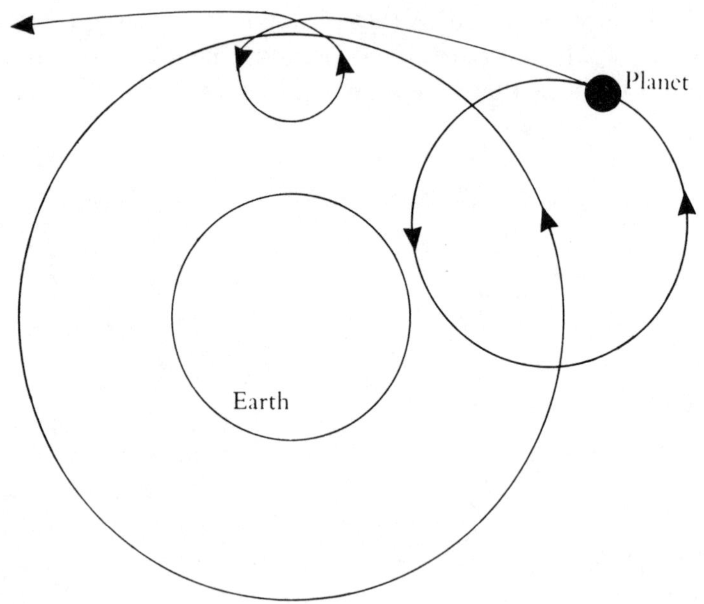

Figure 1.4

other points it will appear to be moving backwards. By careful geometrical construction of circles and epicycles Ptolemy was able to plot orbits for each of the planets that explained their observed motions. Ptolemy's book, *Almagest*, remained the standard astronomical reference until the beginning of the seventeenth century. Even Copernicus made use of Ptolemy's data.

These two examples of Greek scientific achievement allow us a rough understanding of the nature of theory. To repeat: a theory is not just another statement or speculation about the facts, but is a systematic attempt to describe, explain, and organize facts. From a contemporary point of view Greek science is woefully inadequate. Ptolemy's geocentric planetary theory had to be replaced with a heliocentric theory that was forced to abandon altogether his devices of circles and epicycles. Even Euclid's geometry was full of logical difficulties and had to be substantially reworked. What we must keep before us, however, is not the obvious fact that Greek science was mistaken – the same judgment will doubtless be visited upon our science in the future – but rather the great Greek accomplishment in inventing the very idea of science with its attendant notion of theoretical explanation and understanding.

It has been traditional for intellectual historians to divide Greek philosophy into three periods by making use of the figure of Socrates (ca. 470–399 BC) as the locus of the division. First there is the earlier, pre-Socratic, period, the Socratic period that includes Plato (427–347 BC) and Aristotle (384–322 BC), and a later period that coincides with the spread of Greek ideas around the ancient world with the conquests of Alexander the Great.

The early pre-Socratic philosophy was for the most part concerned with providing descriptions and explanations of the physical world. It wanted to know what things were made of, what the nature of the stars and planets was, how they moved, and the like. We would describe this as more like what we think of as physical science rather than philosophy. In the fifth century, however, Greek thinkers began to apply their newly forged intellectual tools to questions of human concern and especially to questions of ethics and politics. They began to ask how people should live their lives and what the best sort of social and political structure is.

These questions about human concerns are really of two kinds. We can investigate the ways in which people actually do live, catalogue the things they value and choose and describe the various kinds of social relations among people and the structure of the political systems under which they live. Investigations such as these make up a good part of what we now call the social sciences, that is, anthropology, sociology, and political science. The Greeks were certainly interested in these questions and the germ of the social sciences can be found among the Greeks. There was, however, another kind of question that intrigued them. Rather than asking how people do live they wanted to ask how they *ought* to live, how they *ought* to conduct their affairs and what kind of social and political organization is the best. By asking these questions the Greeks invented moral philosophy, that is, ethics and political philosophy.

There was another kind of question that began to be asked in the fifth century. The pioneer Greek scientists had been busy accumulating knowledge about the world. They had learned, for example, many things about the nature of the earth and about the movements of the stars and planets. In answer to the question What do we know? the Greeks could list a great many things. Now they asked questions of an altogether different sort: What is knowledge? What is it to know something? What is the difference between knowing something and merely believing it? These questions are not answered by a list of things that are known, but are questions about the very idea of knowledge or, as we shall say, about the *concept* of knowledge.

This question about a concept is a characteristically philosophical one. In their philosophical capacities philosophers are not concerned to investigate the facts of either the physical world or the world of human affairs – they leave that to the natural scientists and social scientists – but they are concerned to investigate and understand the concepts we use when we talk about and try to understand the world and our lives in it. Philosophers can investigate not only the general concept of knowledge, but moral and ethical concepts as well. In the course of our daily lives we describe people and situations as good or bad and actions as right or wrong. What do we mean when we apply these notions? What is the nature of goodness? What makes a right act right? Is there any more to morality than mere customary usage?

It is questions like these that the Greek philosophers of the fifth century BC began to ask and that we find being discussed systematically and in detail for the first time in the dialogues of Plato written in the fourth century. It was the assumption of Plato as well as other Greek thinkers that we could arrive at a theoretical understanding of these issues about human conduct and human values just as we can arrive at a theoretical understanding of natural and mathematical phenomena.

Although the Greeks investigated philosophical questions about science, mathematics, ethics, and politics, it is worth noting that they never gave much philosophical consideration to religion. This lack of theoretical attention was not because religion was not important to the Greeks, for it certainly was, but it was important to them in very different ways than it was the for the Israelites and those that followed in the religious tradition they created. We can see this importance shown in the plots of the Greek tragic dramas which were almost invariably based on difficulties in the relationships between men and the gods and it was very important for the Greeks to take part in the various public and private rituals in honor of the gods. But, unlike the Jews, the Greeks were polytheists.[8] The Greeks worshipped many different gods and they were fully aware that other people worshipped many different gods, but there was never any sense among the Greeks that there was competition between all these different gods and their worshippers. By and large the ancient world felt no need to proselytize or convert others to any particular form of worship.

Nor did the Greeks have anything like scripture. The closest they came to it was in poetry. It was on the great epic poems of Homer, the *Iliad* and *Odyssey*, and works such as Hesiod's *Theogony*[9] that the Greeks relied for their knowledge of the gods. The reading and memorization of this poetry made up a large portion of Greek education and it was from these tales that children learned of the heroes whose conduct they were to imitate. As Sunday school children learn about courage from the story of David and Goliath so Greek lads learned about courage and heroism from Homer's tales of Achilles and the other heroes. Every ancient culture had its myths and stories of creation. The one that is best known to us is the Hebrew book of origins that we know under its Greek title, Genesis. Most of these stories tell how the gods made the world, usually out of pre-existing material,[10] and often with the cooperation of the goddesses. Hesiod begins his poem of creation this way:

> The first power to come into being was Chaos. Then arose Gaia,
> broad-bosomed earth, which serves as the ever-immovable base for
> all the immortals who dwell on the peaks of snowy Olympos;
> and then shadowy Tartaros deep in the wide-wade earth;
> and then Eros surpassing every immortal in beauty,
> who, a loosener of limbs, brings all immortals and mortals under
> his power and makes them unable to think as they should.
> And out of Chaos black Night and Erebos came into being,
> and out of night then came the brightness of Aither and Day,
> whom she conceived by lying in love and mingling with Erebos.[11]

It has been argued that the earliest Greek scientific theorizing about the nature of the world was the result of dissatisfaction with mythologies such as Hesiod's and a desire to replace them with more rational explanations of what the world is like and how it got that way. In these new proto-scientific theories the roles that had been played by the gods were assigned to various natural elements and forces. If this is true, then there was a dispute between science and religion right from the beginning of science and philosophy. Despite a couple of disparaging remarks about religious beliefs preserved in the fragments of the earliest thinkers and despite the fact that more than one philosopher got into trouble with the authorities for espousing scientific views that were considered sacrilege, the tolerant polytheism of the Greeks never provided them with the motivation to investigate religion systematically.

It would only be much later when the world had become a very different place that the intellectual resources of Greek science and philosophy would be applied to matters of religion. And that application had to wait until a unique conception of religion had been developed in another part of the ancient world. This religious conception had its origins with the ancient Israelites.

The Israelites, the Jews, and God

The Israelites were a Semitic people who were nomadic desert dwellers. In a series of migrations they moved into an area west of the Jordan river in the ancient near east during the latter half of the second millennium BC, the last invasion occurring most probably during the thirteenth century BC. This was the land that came to be known as Palestine. They lived under some kind of loosely federated tribal organization and rarely acted in a coordinated fashion. A part of this group may have escaped from a condition of serfdom in Egypt not long before.

Their migrations into Palestine brought them into conflict with the people already living there, the Canaanites. In some instances the Canaanites were defeated and killed and in others they simply lived and mingled with one another. The Israelites borrowed much from the Canaanites including their language, Hebrew. As soon as they had established themselves in the land west of the Jordan they were faced with another conflict. A commercial and city-dwelling people known as the Philistines had established themselves in various towns along the Mediterranean coast and were threatening the position of the Israelites. It was the Philistines who gave their name to Palestine. To meet this threat it was clear that the Israelites were going to need a stronger and more centralized political organization than the traditional tribal arrangement afforded.

It was as the result of this need that Saul became the first king of Israel about 1020 BC. The Philistines were defeated and the Israelites were more or less masters of the land. Saul's shaky rule was consolidated by his protégé David who ruled from 1000 to 961. The kingdom reached its greatest extent and strength under David's son, Solomon. Solomon died in 922 and his kingdom died with him. What had been a united kingdom was now split into a northern and a southern half. The northern kingdom was known as Israel and the southern was called Judah.

The two small kingdoms lived a precarious existence between Egypt and Assyria, the great powers of the day. The northern kingdom fell to the Assyrians in 722 and ceased to exist. It was this debacle that gave rise to the myth of the lost tribes of Israel. There is no mystery about it; they simply lost their identity as Israelites. Judah managed to maintain its independence for a while longer until it was conquered in 587 by the Babylonians, a new power in the mideast.

The conquest had pretty well devastated the capital city of Jerusalem and a number of prominent people had been taken to Babylon as hostages. This is the period that is called the Babylonian Captivity. This came to an end when Babylonia was defeated in its turn by the new Persian empire. The Persians permitted the hostage groups to return and the kingdom of Judah was reestablished after a fashion and was permitted some autonomy within the Persian empire which had by then extended its control over most of the ancient near east. It was at this time that the people we have been calling the Israelites came to be known as Jews, a name derived from Judah.

Judah would once more fall victim to the latest newcomer among the great powers. This time it was the empire of Alexander the Great. Alexander conquered all of the ancient near east in the period 336–323 BC. His successors ruled the Jews until the Maccabean revolt of the 160s brought a new period of stormy independence. This independence was snuffed out for good by the Roman conquest of the first century BC, when Judea became a minor addendum to the Roman Empire.

The early Israelites were probably little different from the other peoples of their time. There is no reason to believe that they were not polytheists like everyone else, but after a time one deity begins to be more and more important. He is known to us as Yahweh. The name is curious and interesting. The old Hebrew did not use vowels in its writing and the name was written YHWH. It is possible that the name is derived from a form of the verb "to be." Remember that God told Moses his name was "I am that I am" (Exodus 3:14). The familiar name, Jehovah, is apparently a medieval corruption of Yahweh. He was sometimes referred to as Elohim, "El" being a common Semitic name applied to any god. The name Yahweh (YHWH) was thought to be too sacred to be pronounced, but it could be written. Instead He was frequently called Adonai, usually translated as "Lord."

There is little, if any, suggestion of monotheism in the first five books of the Bible. This group of books is called in Greek the Pentateuch, the five books or scrolls, and is called Torah, teaching, by the Jews. Yahweh issues the commandment that "You shall have no other gods besides Me" (Exodus 20:3 and Deuteronomy 5:7) and tells Moses that "you must not worship any other god, because the LORD, whose name is Impassioned, is an impassioned God" (Exodus 34:14).[12] These commandments do not deny that there are other gods, but insist only that it is Yahweh who is to be worshipped by the Israelites.

In the early books of the Bible Yahweh is really only another character in the stories. He walks in the garden 'in the breezy time of the day' and he has to ask Adam where he is (Genesis 3:8–9). He has a meal with Abraham at his tent and walks with Abraham toward Sodom because He wants to see for himself if the place is as wicked as has been reported. Abraham then tries to talk Yahweh out of destroying the place, but is obviously not successful (Genesis 18). Yahweh speaks to Moses "face to face, as one man speaks to another" (Exodus 33:11), but on another occasion permits Moses to see only His back, not His face (Exodus 33:23).

Yahweh is not the God of all peoples, but has attachments to particular individuals. He makes a covenant with Abraham which is supposed to apply not only to Abraham, but to all Abraham's descendants as well (Genesis 17), yet nothing is said about anybody else. He tells Isaac that He is "the God of your father Abraham" (Genesis 26:24) and later introduces Himself to Moses as "the God of Abraham, the God of Isaac, and the God of Jacob" (Exodus 3:6). In all of these dealings and introductions there is, once more, no suggestion of monotheism. Time and again Yahweh insists to someone that He is *that* person's God and the one *that* person is to worship. The implication is clear that other people and other nations have their own gods, but Yahweh's favorites are not to worship them.

The establishment of the kingdom that replaced the old tribal federation introduced centralized government to Israel and it was only natural that the worship of Yahweh, which was becoming the national religion, would also become centralized. The power of the monarchy was centered in the capital, Jerusalem, and the Yahweh religion also became centered there in the great temple built by Solomon.

When the Babylonians conquered the kingdom of Judah in 587 BC the Yahweh religion of ancient Israel underwent a crisis. The city of Jerusalem was largely destroyed in the conquest and along with it Solomon's temple. Some number of prominent Israelites were taken to Babylon as hostages. How could Yahweh be worshipped now that His temple no longer existed? How could He be worshipped in a foreign land when His powers were essentially local? These were the questions that the victims of the Babylonian Captivity had to face and they gave these questions magnificent literary expression in the Psalms:

> By the rivers of Babylon,
> there we sat,
> sat and wept,
> as we thought of Zion.
> There on the poplars
> we hung up our lyres,
> for our captors asked us there for songs,
> our tormentors, for amusement,
> "Sing us one of the songs of Zion."
> How can we sing a song of the LORD on alien soil?
>
> (*Psalm 137*)

As a result of this crisis a new conception of Yahweh began to emerge. By the end of the Babylonian Captivity Judaism is unequivocally monotheist and Yahweh is no longer only the deity of a local people, but is well on His way to becoming the God of the whole world who can be worshipped anywhere. This new view of God can be found in the prophets who wrote during the captivity and the century after the return to Jerusalem and the construction of the second temple. The so-called Second Isaiah[13] has God say, "I am the LORD and there is none else; / Beside Me there is no god" (Isaiah 45:5). This claim to be the only God is repeated several times.

Yahweh is also quoted as saying, "The heaven is My throne / and the earth is My footstool: / Where could you build a house for Me, / What place could serve as My abode?" (Isaiah 66:1). God's rhetorical question suggests that He does not dwell in one place, but is, as later theology would have it, omnipresent, everywhere. God is becoming a transcendent deity, that is, He is not part of the world and is not to be thought of as another thing or person in the world.

This new conception of God allows us to realize an interesting philosophical aspect of the old prohibitions against making images of God in Exodus 20, Deuteronomy 5, and several other places. Like as not the injunction against representations of God was intended to keep the religious practices of the Israelites distinct from those of the Canaanites whom they were trying conquer. The use of sacred images and idols figured prominently in the Canaanite religion and there was the constant danger that the Israelites would adopt the customs of the people they were seeking to conquer. As long as Yahweh appeared simply as one of the characters in the story, walking in the garden and so on, then making a statue in His likeness would be an altogether feasible project. The prohibition, then, presupposes that it could be done, but forbids you to do it.

If, however, God is transcendent and not a thing in the world, then there is nothing that could be captured by a likeness or a portrait. It becomes impossible to say what God looks like, how tall He is, whether He is thin or fat and so on. Even if we wanted to, it would be impossible to make a likeness of God.

We must understand this last point correctly. If God is transcendent and not of this world, then none of the physical descriptions that apply to human beings apply to God. When we try to describe something in terms that do not apply to that kind of thing the result is nonsense. Suppose we describe Mary as six feet tall. Let us suppose that she is only five feet tall. In that case the description is false. The description nevertheless makes sense because people are the kinds of things that have height. Let us now change the example and describe Mary as in the key of E major. The sentence "Mary is in the key of E major" makes no literal sense because key designations apply to music, but not to people. It is like that with God and any attempt to describe God in the kind of language that applies to the physical characteristics of people can result only in nonsense.

Earlier in this chapter it was said that one important interest of philosophy was a concern for concepts and a concern for concepts is in large measure a concern for what it makes sense to say about things. The post-Exilic Jews had a different concept of God from that of the earlier Israelites, and that entails that they had to talk about God differently. In this light the commandment "You shall not make for yourself a sculptured image" can be understood as a remark about the concept of God to the effect that there is nothing that can count as an image of God because none of the physical descriptions of things in this world and the representations that can be made of them have any application to God.

Let us not suppose that the Jews thought that the commandment made this conceptual, i.e. philosophical, point for they did not. Philosophy was not in the repertoire of the older Israelites or the Jews of the period we have been talking about. The Jews possessed neither science nor philosophy. The period of the Babylonian Exile that gave rise to the new ideas about God coincided exactly with the time that the Greeks were beginning their work in science and philosophy, but the interests and talents of the two peoples were vastly different. There were those among the Greeks who were driven to search for rational explanations of both natural and human phenomena. If there were such among the Jews we do not hear of them until much later when some Jews began to be influenced by Greek culture.

The Jewish attitude to the kind of inquiries that the Greeks would insist upon is perhaps best represented in the Book of Job. Job is described as blameless and upright, yet he is made to suffer the loss of his possessions and his children and to suffer disgusting bodily afflictions. The reason why these things befall Job, as stated in the first two chapters, will appear curious to any careful reader of the story, but that is not now our concern. The question for Job arises because God's law had stated that those who are righteous and blameless and who obey the law will prosper. Job satisfies those conditions – it is a premise of the story – but he suffers rather than prospers. Why should this be so? The answer that God gives to this question, in disregard of the opening chapters, is that He created the world, rules the world, makes things happen as they do and, since man cannot understand the ways of God, it is not his place to ask such questions. Man's duty is simply to bow before the power of God.

There is no attempt in any of this to seek a theoretical account of the relation between God and the world that would explain Job's, or anyone else's, situation. If we assume that Job represented the characteristic Judaic attitude, then it is clear that it is a stance that effectively discourages asking the kind of questions that were characteristic of Greek thought.

Christianity and Philosophy

With the spread of Christianity, however, there were important intellectual changes. The first Christians were, of course, Jews and in its beginnings Christianity was merely a cult within Judaism. Within a very short time, however, there was a split within the new movement between those who wished to maintain its Jewish nature and those who wished to encourage non-Jews to become Christians without also having to become Jews. As we know, the latter party won the day and the original Jewish Christianity passed from history.

The non-Jewish world into which early Christianity sought to expand was the world of the Roman Empire. It was also a world which had considerable acquaintance with Greek ideas. The Greeks had long ago established cities and colonies at many places around the Mediterranean Sea. When the Romans began the expansion that eventually turned a minor Italian city state into a world empire they came into contact with the Greeks and were taken with their literature, art, science, and philosophy.

Since the Romans had little of this kind of culture of their own, they were quick to borrow it from the Greeks. In addition, the conquests of Alexander the Great in the fourth century BC spread at least a veneer of Greek culture over all of the ancient near east. In time Greece itself and much of the near east were incorporated into the Roman Empire.

Over the centuries the Israelites and the Jews had to defend their national integrity against foreign domination, but they never had to defend their religion against the challenge of other religions. Judaism was the religion of a nation and the Jews never sought to convince others that they should adopt it. It was quite different with Christianity. The Christians were not a nation or political entity struggling either to achieve or to maintain independence. They were for the most part citizens of the Roman Empire and they were trying to convince other Romans to become Christians. They had a lot of competition since there were many religions competing for the allegiance of people living within and on the boundaries of the empire.

In order to win converts in the wider Roman world Christianity had to do two things. It had to provide explanations and justifications of its doctrines to the world at large and it also had to clarify and determine for itself exactly what those doctrines were. Thus was born the need for systematic theology.[14] Undoubtedly the most urgent of those doctrines concerned the nature of Jesus who was called the Christ. All Christians agreed that Jesus stood in some special relation to God, but there was no agreement about what this relation was. Some believed that Jesus was simply a man who was inspired by God, others thought that he was God himself and his human form was only an illusion, and still others that he was both man and God.

In its early centuries Christianity met with considerable hostility and from time to time was subject to persecutions of greater or less severity. A turning point came in the first part of the fourth century AD when the emperor Constantine became a convert to Christianity and began the process that would make Christianity the official religion of the empire. Constantine was disturbed by the fact that there was little unity within Christianity and little agreement about its doctrines. This would not do for a religion that was to be an adjunct of a unified empire. A series of church councils was convened, most notably the Council of Nicea in AD 325, to determine what doctrines were to be accepted as orthodoxy, i.e. "right doctrine." It was at these councils that the doctrine of the Trinity was formulated and the various creeds adopted.

It was because of these very practical needs that Christian beliefs were developed theoretically. The theological development of doctrine and its rational justification required an intellectual framework; Christianity would find one ready to hand in the form of Greek philosophy, and every educated person in the ancient world could be counted on to have at least some degree of familiarity with its ideas. It was in these early Christian centuries that the interplay between philosophy and religion began and it is from this time that we can date the beginning of the philosophy of religion.[15]

The doctrine of the Trinity is expressed in what has become known as the Nicene Creed. The Nicene Creed begins in this way:

> I believe in one God, the Father almighty, maker of heaven and earth, of all things visible and invisible; and in one Lord Jesus Christ, the only-begotten Son of God, begotten from the Father before all ages, light from light, true God

> from true God, begotten not made, of one substance with Father.

In this rather formidable passage we can see clearly how Christianity made use of the Greek philosophical notion of *substance* to explain how Jesus as the Son can be identified with God the Father. They are separate yet somehow the same, of the same substance, that is, the same stuff. Fortunately, however, we do not have to pause to make sense out of the notion. It is enough to note it as an example of the influence of Greek philosophy on Christianity.

The two greatest figures in ancient philosophy were Plato (427–347 BC) and Aristotle (384–322 BC). It was the philosophy of Plato that was most influential in the formation of theological doctrines in Christianity's early centuries although it was Aristotle whose thought would become the dominant force much later in the middle ages.

It was not so much the writings of Plato themselves that the early Christian philosophers studied, but the work of Plato as mediated by a school of philosophy that we know as Neo-Platonism. Neo-Platonism is associated with the Greek philosopher Plotinus who lived in Alexandria in Egypt in the middle of the third century AD. Plotinus produced a mystical version of Plato in which everything was thought of as an emanation from what he called the One who was the source of all existence, goodness, truth, and perfection. It was easy enough for Christian thinkers to identify Plotinus' One with God, but we do not have to stop to worry about the details of all that. The first great Christian philosopher was St Augustine (AD 354–430). After his conversion to Christianity Augustine eventally became bishop of Hippo in North Africa and was very much influenced by Neo-Platonism.[16]

In the fourth century the emperor Constantine had found the government of the vast Roman Empire becoming ever more cumbersome and in the name of administrative efficiency divided the empire into two parts. The western half of the empire was ruled from the traditional capital at Rome, while in the east Constantine rebuilt the old Greek city of Byzantium and renamed it after himself, Constantinople, to be the seat of the eastern empire.

The western empire was suffering from a variety of ailments; there was a general economic decline and numerous Germanic tribes, the barbarians, were moving from central Europe across the frontiers and changing the old Roman ways for ever. By the second half of the fifth century centralized government in the west had collapsed altogether and with it went much of the art, culture, and intellectual life of the ancient world. Population declined and municipal services, water supply, sewers, and the like, ceased to function. Europe entered on those centuries that can be truly characterized as the Dark Ages when life indeed tended to be nasty, brutish, and short.

The eastern empire was able to retain its integrity and would survive, although with ever shrinking boundaries, until the middle of the fifteenth century. Many of the economic and cultural links between east and west, however, were broken. The church was divided with the western churches looking more and more to the bishop at Rome for leadership while the eastern churches took their lead from the bishop at Constantinople. The knowledge of the Greek language tended to disappear in the west and with it went the knowledge of Greek science and philosophy. For several centuries Plato and Aristotle were not much more than names to people in the west.

But by AD 1000 the prospects for Europe were getting brighter. The barbarian invasions were over and a certain amount of economic prosperity was returning. Great new buildings, especially churches, were going up everywhere for this was the beginning of the Romanesque style in architecture. Schools had been established and there was now that measure of safety and security that make a life of scholarship and intellectual inquiry possible. Philosophy made a new beginning and the major influence on it was Neo-Platonism as Christianized by St Augustine.

By the middle of the twelfth century, however, the works of Aristotle were being recovered by the west. The story of this recovery is a fascinating intellectual odyssey. While the collapse of the Roman Empire in the west and the advent of the Dark Ages saw science and philosophy virtually disappear, the tradition of Greek thought was continued in the east. Meanwhile in Arabia Muhammad had succeeded in imposing both the new religion of Islam and a measure of political unity on the warring tribes there. Now that they were no longer wasting their energies fighting one another, their strength was directed toward external conquest. By the eighth century the Arabs had expanded into much of the ancient near east, into Egypt, across North Africa, and into Sicily and Spain.

In the east they had seized much of the territory of the eastern Roman Empire and there they met the schools of Greek science and philosophy. They were fascinated by this discovery and soon the works of Aristotle and others were translated into Arabic and intensely studied. It was not long before the Arabs began to make important contributions to sciences such as mathematics, optics, and medicine. During the middle ages Islamic science and philosophy were far ahead of anything known in the west.

Schools of science and philosophy were established at many places throughout the Islamic world. There were also important schools of Jewish philosophy. The Arabs treated the Jews with far more tolerance than the Christians and generally the Jews were quick to welcome Islamic rule in exchange for Christian domination. Many Jews rose to positions of power and influence in Islamic society and politics. Like their Christian counterparts, both Arab and Jewish philosophers sought to use Greek philosophy and science to provide rational explanations and justifications of their religious beliefs.

There were important schools of both Arabic and Jewish philosophy in Spain and it was largely by contacts with Spain that the west came to rediscover its almost forgotten Greek heritage. The texts of Artistotle made their way into the west in the twelfth century. Aristotle was translated into Latin from the Arabic version or in some cases from the Hebrew version. By the thirteenth century, however, much improved translations were available from the original Greek.

The rediscovery of Aristotle was a remarkably exciting event for western philosophers. Aristotle had written on just about every subject of importance, logic, metaphysics, ethics, politics, poetry, physics, astronomy, biology, and psychology. Suddenly a whole world of intellectual accomplishment was opened up that the west had not even known existed. It was not long before Aristotelian modes of thought took over from the Augustinian version of Neo-Platonism of the earlier middle ages.In the next chapter we will trace in some detail this Greek influence on two important philosophers of the middle ages, St Anselm of Canterbury and St Thomas Aquinas.

Suggestions for Further Reading

The Greeks

The most complete general history of Greek philosophy is W. K. C. Guthrie, *A History of Greek Philosophy* (Cambridge: Cambridge University Press, 1962). For a detailed history of the earliest period of Greek philosophy see F. M. Cornford, *From Religion to Philosophy* (New York: Harper Torchbooks, 1957; originally published 1912), *Principium Sapientiae* (Cambridge: Cambridge University Press, 1952), and G. S. Kirk and J. E. Raven, *The Presocratic Philosophers* (Cambridge: Cambridge University Press, 1960).

My account of Greek astronomy relies upon Stephen Toulmin and June Goodfield, *The Fabric of the Heavens* (New York: Harper Torchbooks, 1961). This is a very informative and very readable history of astronomy and mechanics from the ancient world to Isaac Newton. Charles Singer's *A Short History of Scientific Ideas* (Oxford: Clarendon Press, 1959) is also useful. For an account of what we think the Egyptians knew about geometry see Florian Cajori, *A History of Elementary Mathematics* (New York: Macmillan, 1914). A useful brief account of the work of Euclid and the development of non-Euclidean geometry can be found in Leonard M. Blumenthal, *A Modern View of Geometry* (San Francisco and London: W. H. Freeman and Co., 1961).

The best general introduction to Greek history and culture is Will Durant's *The Life of Greece* (New York: Simon & Schuster, 1939).

Jewish origins

For those interested in the political and religious history of Israel, Abraham Leon Sacher's *A History of the Jews*, 5th edn revised (New York: Alfred A. Knopf, 1967), and Harry M. Buck's *People of the Lord* (New York: Macmillan, 1966) are good places to get started.

Christian origins

Kenneth Scott Latourette's *A History of the Expansion of Christianity*, vol. 1, *The First Five Centuries* (New York and London: Harper & Bros, 1937), is a standard reference for this period. Martin E. Marty's *A Short History of Christianity* offers a good summary of Christian origins. *The Oxford Illustrated History of Christianity*, ed. John McManners (Oxford and New York: Oxford University Press, 1991), is also highly recommended. Will Durant's eminently readable *Caesar and Christ* (New York: Simon & Schuster, 1944) is a fascinating account of the Roman world in which Christianity emerged.

Christian and medieval philosophy

There are many histories of medieval philosophy. Etienne Gilson's *The Christian Philosophy of Saint Augustine* (New York: Random House, Vintage Books, 1967) and *History of Christian Philosophy in the Middle Ages* (New York: Random House, 1955) are good sources. Also useful are Maurice De Wulf, *History of Medieval Philosophy* (New York, Bombay, and Calcutta: Longmans, Green, and Co., 1909), and Armand Maurer, *Medieval Philosophy* (New York: Random House, 1962).

Notes

1 I am deliberately ignoring intellectual developments in ancient India and China that can be described as philosophical or scientific. Whatever these were, they had little, if any, influence on Greek and subsequent European thought. In any event the intellectual spirit of these cultures was very different from that of the Greeks. As the great scholar of Indian philosophy, Heinrich Zimmer, put it, "The chief aim of Indian thought is to unveil and integrate into consciousness what has been thus resisted and hidden by the forces of life – not to explore and describe the visible

world" (*Philosophies of India* (New York: Pantheon Books, 1951), p. 3).

2 Given this frame of mind much science has to be dismissed as a fraud perpetrated by scientists who don't really know what they are talking about and who insult our common sense by trying to convince us that there really are little things too small for anyone ever to see. It is curious how much of this attitude has found its way into certain modes of thinking about religion. Of this more later.

3 There is a very real historical question about how much of the *Elements* was Euclid's original work and how much was borrowed from the work of others. It is likely that some of the books of the *Elements* itself were not written by Euclid. These questions, however, need not detain us. What is important for us is the theoretical achievement that the name "Euclid" has come to represent.

4 For some two hundred years mathematicians have challenged one or more of Euclid's postulates and created several systems of alternative, non-Euclidean, geometries. These systems nevertheless are concerned to prove theorems from within the assumptions of the systems and to demonstrate the logical connections between the propositions of the system.

5 There is a certain amount of controversy among philosophers of science about the nature of theories. The reader may wish to consult Ernst Nagel, *The Structure of Science* (New York: Harcourt, Brace & World, 1961), for a detailed discussion of theories and what they are all about.

6 Early on the hypothesis that the heavens may have a controlling influence upon human destiny was not an unreasonable one, but with greater scientific understanding of how things actually act upon one another there is no doubt that the persistence of astrology has to rank as one of the great intellectual frauds of the ages. We should remind ourselves that one inhabitant of the White House was rumored to have regularly consulted an astrologer.

7 You will want to ask yourself why you should believe that the earth rotates upon its axis. It is not an answer to say that you read it in a book for then you will have to ask how the chap who wrote the book found it out.

8 The Greek word for "god" is *theos*, and *poly*, of course, means "many" so polytheism is the belief in many gods. Polytheism may be contrasted with *monotheism*, which is the belief that there is only one god.

9 The suffix of this name is from a Greek word referring to generation or origins. Thus *Theogony* is an account of the generation or origin of the gods.

10 There is nothing in the Genesis accounts that makes explicit that the heaven and earth were created out of nothing rather than pre-existing raw material. The idea of creation out of nothing was a later interpretation.

11 Hesiod, *Theogony*, trans. R. M. Frazer (Norman: University of Oklahoma Press, 1983), 11. 116–125. "Chaos" must be understood here as the chasm that opens to separate heaven and earth which were apparently united at first. The word does not mean disorder. See Frazer's comment, p. 30.

12 All translations from the Old Testament are from *Tanakh, The Holy Scriptures: The New JPS Translation According to the traditional Hebrew Text* (Philadelphia and New York: The Jewish Publication Society, 1988). While it may not have the literary familiarity of the King James version and its descendants, it is more faithful to the original and more aware of textual and translational problems. We should be careful in our use of the name "Old Testament." The distinction between the Old and the New Testaments is a Christian one and carries the implication that the testament or covenant with God established in the Hebrew scriptures is out of date and must be replaced by a new arrangement. This, of course, is an insult to the Jews, for whom the "Old Testament" just is the Bible, the Book.

13 It is generally agreed that the book we know as Isaiah is the work of two pens. The work of the "Second Isaiah" begins

at chapter 40 and was probably written during the period of the exile.

14 The suffix of this word is derived from the Greek *logos* which has several meanings, e.g. "word," "discourse," "definition." Aristotle called an argument a *logos* and the study of argument has thus come to be called logic. Theology, then, is discourse about God. It would not be misleading to say that it means "God theory."

15 It would not be proper to ignore Philo (ca. 30 BC to AD 50), a thoroughly Hellenized (i.e. "Greekified") Jew of Alexandria in Egypt. Philo made use of current Greek philosophical ideas to construct an elaborate system around the idea of God as utterly transcendent. Philo's work, however, is not part of our story.

16 St Augustine tells us of his early life and conversion to Christianity in his *Confessions*. This is one of the great literary works of the western world and should not be missed.

2

The Existence of God

The Existence of God and the Existence of Other Things

In the last chapter we traced the invention of science and philosophy by the Greeks and the development of the concept of God by the Israelites and Jews and pointed out how the Christian use of Jewish religious ideas led to a meeting of religion and philosophy. In this chapter we will begin to investigate the question that many people believe is the central question for the philosophy of religion: Does God exist?

The focus of both Judaism and Christianity is the belief in God and the belief that God has created the world and has taken an active part in the affairs of the world. It would seem vitally important for the religious person to know whether this belief is true or false. If it is true, then the person's religious belief is justified and, if it is false, then that belief is a delusion.

How are we to determine whether or not there is a God? Let's start by asking how we determine whether or not there is anything of a particular sort. Is there an extra chair in the next room? Is there really a Loch Ness monster? Is there really such a thing as a quark? Is there a prime number between 17 and 23? We have no difficulty in answering the first question. Go into the next room and look. You know what a chair looks like. The search for Nessie does pose some difficulties. The loch is deep and dark and we don't really quite know what we are looking for. But with enough time and expense the place could be searched thoroughly enough either to turn up something unusual enough to satisfy us or to make clear that there is nothing big and finny lurking there.

Quarks, however, are a different matter. They are not the sort of thing that you can see, even in a good light, since they are smaller than light waves. Quarks are unlike chairs and monsters in that the idea of a quark is part of atomic theory and to know what a quark is, or what it is supposed to be, you have to understand that theory. The ordinary objects of our everyday world – and if monsters are not ordinary things they are, at any rate, just odd sorts of big things – are not the materials of theory. You do not have to know a theory to know what a chair is or to be frightened by something that sticks its head out of the water. We do not look to see whether there are any quarks. Physicists verify the existence of quarks by using the theory to predict changes in energy levels in appropriate laboratory experiments. If the predicted energy emissions actually show up, then physicists say they have verified the existence of the particles.

Whether there is a prime number between two other numbers is a very different kind of question from the first three. We answer the question not by looking to see or by making predictions to be tested by experiments in the laboratory, but instead by constructing a mathematical proof. In this case it is a very simple one, but there are other cases where it is most complex.

The first three questions are what philosophers call *empirical* questions and that means they are questions that must be answered by using one or more of our five senses. In order to answer them we must make *observations* and frequently our sense observations must be aided by various scientific instruments, microscopes, telescopes, galvanometers, and the like.[1] The question about the prime number is obviously not an empirical question. To answer it we do not observe, but use reason to construct a proof.

What about the existence of God? Adam, had he but taken a course in philosophy, could have said that the question of Yahweh's existence is an empirical matter; after all, he saw Him and spoke with Him. Given the assumptions of the post-Exilic conception of God, however, Adam's claim would have to be disputed. God is now thought of as transcendent and not part of the physical world; He has no physical properties. Since the only things that our senses can observe are things in the physical world, it follows that we cannot observe God. If that is the case, then it is clear that the question of the existence of God is not an empirical question, at least not in any obvious sense.

Suppose someone doubts that there is a God. How might we go about convincing that person that God really does exist? One way is ruled out from the start: we cannot point Him out and say, "See, there He is." This failure of an empirical approach may suggest that settling the question may be akin to settling the question about the prime number. What we need is not observation, but perhaps reasoning and something akin to mathematical proof. A proof in mathematics is a kind of *argument* and we must pause here to say something about the notion of an argument.

The Nature of Argument

The word "argument" has several meanings and we must sort them out so as not to misunderstand what we are about. When we speak of an argument what more than likely comes to mind is a dispute or even a quarrel or spat. Another interesting use of the word is to denote the value of a variable in a function. Thus we can say that the value of the function 2x is 8 for the argument 4, 10 for the argument 5, and so on. A third sense, although one not much met with these days, understands an argument as a synopsis or abstract of some longer piece of work.

The meaning of the word "argument" that we will be investigating and using here is not any of the above. When we speak of an argument we will mean an example of reasoning. To argue is to give reasons for supposing that what someone believes or says is true. An argument consists of two or more propositions; the proposition whose truth is to be established is called the *conclusion* and the propositions that state the reasons in support of the conclusion are called the *premises*. Consider this sample of an argument:

(1) All men are mortal.
(2) All Greeks are men.
(3) Therefore, all Greeks are mortal.

(1) and (2) are the premises and (3) is the conclusion. When we examine arguments we shall follow the convention of

listing the premises first and then the conclusion and we will separate the premises from the conclusion by a line.

We have just introduced the term *proposition* and that must be explained before we go on. Consider these sentences: "It is raining," "Rain is falling," "Il pleut," "Es regnet." These four sentences obviously have something in common – they all say the same thing, or, as we shall put it, they all express or assert the same proposition. A proposition is either *true* or *false*. A proposition can, in fact, be characterized as whatever can be either true or false. We must be careful to distinguish sentences which are used to ask questions, give orders, or make exclamations from those that are used to assert propositions. Interrogatives, imperatives, and exclamations cannot, of course, be either true or false.

The systematic study of arguments is logic. Logicians have traditionally divided arguments into *deductive* and *inductive* arguments. Deductive arguments can be classified as *valid* or *invalid*. Let's look again at our argument that all Greeks are mortal. The argument is valid. The conclusion follows logically from the premises, that is, if the premises of this argument are true, then the conclusion *must* be true. Let's make a change in the premises of the argument:

All fish are mortal.
All Greeks are fish.
____
Therefore, all Greeks are mortal.

The result is still a valid argument. But let's make another change:

All fish are mortal.
All Irishmen are fish.
____
All Irishmen are mortal.

This change still leaves us with a valid argument. Now for one final change.

All fish are taxidermists.
All Irishmen are fish.
All Irishmen are taxidermists.

Again the result is a valid argument. This should help us see that the validity of an argument does not depend upon the truth of the premises, but only upon the *form* of the argument. The argument we have been using as a sample has this form:

All A is B.
All C is A.
All C is B.

The letters A, B, and C function here as variables. It makes no difference what terms we substitute for them; the result will always be a valid argument. There is an indefinitely large number of possible argument forms and the study of them is that part of logic called formal logic. To repeat: a valid deductive argument is an argument in which, if the premises are true, the conclusion must be true. We can put this by saying that in a valid deductive argument either the conclusion can be deduced from the premises or the premises entail the conclusion.[2] We should note that if an argument is invalid it does not follow that its conclusion is necessarily false. An invalid argument may have a true conclusion; it is just that you cannot establish the conclusion from the premises of that argument.

The truth of the premises of an inductive argument do not entail the truth of its conclusion, but instead create a greater or less probability that the conclusion is true. Let us suppose that the great detective at the scene of the crime reasons in this way:

> The bloody knife was found in the butler's room.
> The butler was heard to mutter threats against the master at the local.
> The butler cannot account for his whereabouts on the fatal night.
> ____________________
> The butler is the murderer.

These three premises do not entail that the butler did it, but they do create a presumption and lend probability to the accusation. The premises can all be true and yet the conclusion be false. The bloody knife may have been planted by the real murderer; the anger at the master may have been only of a passing moment; and he may have been in a certain intimate situation with the mistress and refuses to say anything that would compromise her.

Any conclusion based upon a sampling procedure, a political poll, for example, is an inductive argument. If the sample is well chosen, then what is true of the sample will probably, but not necessarily, be true of the entire population. Strictly speaking, then, inductive arguments cannot be evaluated as either valid or invalid. They can be described as stronger or weaker depending upon how well they make the case for the truth of the conclusion.

In all that follows we will spend a good bit of time examining and evaluating arguments. When we evaluate an argument we will follow several steps by asking these questions. (1) Is the argument intended to be deductive or inductive? (2) If it is deductive, is the argument valid? If it is not valid, it can be dismissed right away. (3) If it is valid, are the premises true? If the premises are not true, it obviously cannot establish its conclusion. A deductive argument that is valid and whose premises are true is said to be *sound*. (4) If the argument is intended to be inductive we will still want to ask whether the premises are true. (5) If they are true, then we must ask whether they are relevant to the truth of the conclusion and whether they provide enough support to lend a reasonable degree of probability to the conclusion.

Reasons for Believing that God Exists

With these preliminaries about arguments in mind, let's get back to the question about God's existence. How might the existence of God be argued for? What reasons might someone have for believing that the proposition "God exists" is true? Here is a list of some typical answers to that question that many people are inclined to give. The Bible says God exists; God is required to create the world and the order in it; I have had an experience of God or felt Him in my heart; the existence of miracles; belief in God has changed my life; I have been taught that God exists. Let us take each of these reasons in turn and consider them as if each was a premise in deductive argument whose conclusion is "God exists."

> The Bible says that God exists.
> God exists.

It should be clear that the conclusion does not follow from that premise alone. The mere fact that something is written does not in the least guarantee that it is true.[3] To make the argument valid we need another premise that says something like "Whatever the Bible says is true." But why should we suppose that premise is true? It would seem a further argument is needed to establish its truth. That argument might be that, since the Bible is the word of God and God cannot be mistaken, whatever the Bible says is true. Our argument now reads:

> The Bible is the word of God.
> The word of God is always true.
> The Bible says that God exists.
> ___
> God exists.

The argument is now valid, but something has gone wrong. The first premise assumes that God exists, but that is what the argument sets out to establish in the conclusion. This is called circular reasoning: the conclusion is already assumed in the premises. A name for this mistake, or fallacy, is begging the question. This is one of the most blatant examples of begging the question.

In argument form the next reason looks like this:

> There is a world with a very great degree and complexity of order.
> ___
> God exists.

There is no logical connection whatever between the premise and the conclusion. People who offer this reason are inclined to elaborate what they say by adding that God is the only possible explanation for the existence of the world. The revised argument, then, would be:

> If there is a world, then there exists God who created it.
> There is a world.
> ___
> God exists.

This is a valid argument form. Let the letters p and q represent propositions and we see the argument to have this form:[4]

> If p is true, then q is true.
> <u>p is true.</u>
> q is true.

The argument is valid, but is it sound? How do we know that God is required to create the world, that if there is a world there must be a God? This is one of the very things that is denied by non-believers and cannot be accepted without question. One may also be forgiven for raising the possibility that the world was not created at all.

Let's consider now the argument from religious experience.

> <u>I have experienced God (or felt Him in my heart).</u>
> God exists.

If the person has, in fact, experienced *God*, then there is no more need for an argument than there is when I say that there is a salesman at the door; I have seen him. Many people have claimed to have experiences of God, Christ, or the Virgin Mary, among others. There is, however, something very different about such experiences from everyday experiences of seeing people. I saw President Kennedy once and so did several thousand other people who were also in the crowd; it was in the papers and all that. Religious experiences, visions, if you would, are very personal and private; no one else sees what the visionary sees. We want to ask how the person knows who or what was experienced. There is no way to check divine identity as human identity can be checked. We shall not question the sincerity of the person who claims to have such experiences, and such experiences can certainly be important in the religious life of a person. It is just that such claims cannot work as knowledge claims about the existence of God.

On the other hand, if the claim is the more modest one of *feeling* God in one's heart rather than actually *seeing* Him, then we have to ask how it is known that it was God that the person felt and also remark that the existence of a feeling does not entail anything about what exists in the world.

The next argument says

There are miracles.
God exists.

Once more it seems obvious that there is no logical connection between premise and conclusion. Before going on, however, to see how the argument might be repaired, let's note an ambiguity in the word "miracle." What is a miracle? Someone might say that a miracle is an occasion in which God has intervened in the ordinary workings of the world. If that is how the word is understood, then the premise begs the question by smuggling the existence of God into the meaning of the word "miracle." Others sometimes understand a miracle as an event for which there is no known explanation and then go on to argue like this:

Science cannot explain this event.
God caused it (God exists).

This move puts miracles on the same level as Curious Unexplained Phenomena such as are supposed to occur in the Bermuda Triangle or get reported in the UFO magazines. Beware of an argument whose premise says "Either there is a scientific explanation for this or it is the work of God." How do we know these are the alternatives? Instead of saying it is the work of God, why not say it is the result of a time warp in the Bermuda Triangle, of aliens among us or whatever your fancy opts for? This is an instance of a general species of logical mistake that is made when it is argued that since your view is false, inadequate, etc., therefore mine is true. This can be said only when it is known that your view and mine exhaust the possibilities.

Suppose now that this argument is offered:

Belief in God has changed my life.
God exists.

The terms and notions that appear in the conclusion of a deductive argument must already be present in the premises. The conclusion speaks of God, but the premise speaks only of *belief* in God, not God. To make the argument valid, there must be a premise to the effect that whatever I believe in must exist and such a proposition is manifestly false. The fact that religious belief has changed the lives of many people cannot and should not be denied. What is being denied is that the fact can serve as a premise in an argument to the existence of God.

The final reason we will examine here is that I have been taught that God exists. As an argument it looks like this:

I have been taught that God exists.
God exists.

The argument seems to presuppose the unstated premise that whatever I have been taught is true. You do not have to examine your own experience very deeply to realize that this assumption is false. We have all been taught many things that are not true.

All these "reasons" that we have been examining are important and can play important roles in the religious lives of people. What these roles are we will have to talk about later. For the time being, however, it should be clear that, whatever role they play, it is not as premises in arguments whose conclusion is that God exists.

Let us now take a look at some of the historically influential arguments for the existence of God that have been offered by philosophers.

The Philosophers Argue for God

We saw in the last chapter how Greek philosophy and religion came together in Christianity's need to provide an intellectual justification for and defense of its doctrines in the world of the Roman Empire. We saw also how the Dark Ages brought a halt to intellectual life in the west, but in addition how cultural and intellectual life began to flourish once again in the eleventh century. It was to this period that St Anselm (1033–1109) belonged. Anselm was of Italian birth, but later went to England where he became Archbishop of Canterbury.

St Anselm's Argument for the Existence of God

In a little work called the *Proslogian* Anselm gave an argument for the existence of God that has come to be known as the Ontological Argument.[5] This argument is a tough one to get a handle on, but it can teach us some valuable logical lessons. Anselm prefaces his argument with a plea to God to add understanding to the faith that he already has. Anselm has no doubts about the existence of God so the argument is not intended to convince himself, or any other believer, that God exists. It is intended, rather, to clarify the intellectual understanding of God that the believer already has.

Anselm begins his argument with the first verse from Psalm 14 where the fool says there is no God. The fool, of course, is the atheist.[6] The atheist denies that God exists, but in order to deny the existence of something you have to have a conception of what it is that you are denying. Suppose I say that there really is a Santa Claus and you disagree with me and say there is no Santa Claus. In order for there to be a disagreement we have to agree in our conception or definition of Santa Claus. We both have to agree that Santa Claus is, let us say, a fat man who wears a red suit and who lives at the North Pole, etc. I say that there is something fitting that description and you say that nothing satisfies the description. Anselm's definition of God is that God is a being than which nothing greater can be conceived.

This conception of God derives from that developed in post-Exilic Judaism and inherited by Christianity and can be understood as a philosopher's way of describing God as the perfect and absolutely Supreme Being. The fool must understand this definition. Anselm describes the fact that the fool understands the definition of God by saying that the fool has God in his understanding, but does not believe that God exists in reality. To illustrate this he uses the analogy of a painter who has conceived his painting in his understanding although the painting does not yet exist in reality.

Anselm now adds the assumption that whatever exists in the understanding and in reality is greater than whatever exists in the understanding alone. In the light of this the fool has to acknowledge that, if God exists only in the understanding, then He is not a being than which nothing greater can be conceived. To be true to the definition the fool must agree that God also exists in reality. Atheism is thus shown to be contradictory and God must exist.

To get a better understanding of the argument let's represent it just as if it were a proof in geometry where each step in the proof is made explicit and each step is given a justification. It looks like this:

1	God is a being than which nothing greater can be conceived	[Definition]
2	To understand a definition is to have the thing defined in the understanding.	[Assumption]
3	The fool denies that God exists.	[Psalm 14]
4	The fool understands the definition of God.	[Otherwise he couldn't deny His existence]
5	The fool has God in his understanding.	[2, 4]
6	Whatever exists in the understanding and in reality is greater than that which exists in the understanding alone.	[Assumption]
7	For the sake of the argument let us assume that the fool is right and God exists only in	

the understanding, i.e. God
does not exist in reality.

8 Step 7 is inconsistent with 1 and 6. If we accept definition 1, and assumption 6, then 7 must be false.

Therefore:

9 God exists.

The argument is a kind of indirect proof that logicians call *reductio ad absurdum* (reduction to absurdity). In this kind of proof one assumes the contradictory of the proposition that is to be proved and then shows that the assumption entails a contradiction, a false proposition or one that in some way is unacceptable. It is a principle of logic that whatever entails a contradictory or false proposition must itself be false. Anselm wants to prove the proposition that God exists so he allows the fool to assume its denial, that God does not exist. It then turns out that the assumption contradicts itself and so must be false.

The argument is formally valid, that is, if the premises are true, the conclusion must be true. Following the procedure outlined earlier in the chapter we must examine the truth of the premises. Let us not quarrel with the definition of God that Anselm gives us although questions can be raised about it and we must agree that the atheist's position is correctly stated. The problem comes up in premise 5. Anselm assumes that to have an understanding of something, whether it be God, a picture that a painter wants to paint or whatever, is to have that *thing* in the understanding (we may as well say "in the mind"). This is a strange way of talking. We would be inclined to say that rather than having the *thing* in the mind what we have is the *thought*, *idea*, or *notion* of the thing, surely not the thing itself. I understand what a tiger is, but I certainly do not have a tiger in my mind. My mind would then be a dangerous place and I would not want to venture there without taking along at least one green umbrella. That, of course, is absurd.

It is clear, however, that Anselm's argument depends upon the assumption. He has to be thinking that the idea of a thing is a kind of lesser version of the thing itself. Premise 6 is explicit that what is in the understanding and what is in reality are of the same species. Only then would it seem to make sense to compare the item in the mind to the item in reality with respect to greatness. If we substitute the phrase "The fool has an idea of God in his understanding" for "he has God in his understanding," the argument won't work. Ideas and real things can not occupy different places on the same scale of greater and lesser.

Anselm must seem to us the victim of a hopeless confusion, but the assumptions of his argument do follow from a general theory of truth which was very much influenced by some of the ideas of St Augustine. God is thought of as the supreme truth and from this it follows that there is a truth, not only of propositions, but also of thought, of things, of actions, and of will.[7] Not only are propositions and thoughts said to be true, but things are true to the extent to which they exist. Thoughts and things thus supposedly have something in common and this no doubt contributes to the collapse of our ordinary distinction between a thing and the thought of the thing so that Anselm can suppose that it makes sense to say that the fool has God in his understanding. What is interesting for us is not the details of this theory, but the fact that Anselm's argument presupposes a larger philosophical theory. Needless to say, the theory seriously distorts our understanding of the concept of truth.

We may think that the argument, then, begs the question in that the proof of God's existence presupposes the theory of truth that assumes God already exists. But the argument may not be intended to prove anything to the non-believer. Anselm says that faith is required for understanding; the argument is not designed to produce faith. What it does is to show to the believer that the denial of God's existence is contradictory. The fool would not necessarily see that it is contradictory. In order to see that he would have to buy into the theory of truth and then he would have already accepted that God exists. If you do not buy into the metaphysics of truth, then there is no contradiction in the proposition that God does not exist.

Anselm goes on to offer what is sometimes represented as a second argument, but perhaps should be thought of as a corollary of the argument. He says that God cannot be conceived not to exist for whatever can be conceived not to exist cannot be God. In this version the argument was taken up by later thinkers such as René Descartes (1596–1650).

In his *Meditations on First Philosophy* Descartes introduces his argument by reference to a traditional philosophical distinction between *essence* and *existence*. Roughly, the essence of anything is the nature of it and is described in a definition of the thing. The essence of Santa Claus, we may say, is "fat man who wears a red suit and lives at the North Pole, etc."; the essence of a triangle is "three-sided plane figure," and so on. In general the essence of a thing does not entail that the thing exists. There is, alas, no Santa Claus and there need be no triangles. Descartes claims that God is the single exception to this for His essence implies His existence. Descartes conceives of God as the completely perfect being and, since existence is a perfection, He must exist.[8] As a formal argument it looks like this:

> God is the completely perfect being (possesses all perfections).
> Existence is a perfection.
> Therefore, God exists.

We poor finite mortals cannot comprehend all of God's perfections; we could never catalogue them all. But we do know that existence must be one of them. The argument clearly works only in the case of God. Let us try to imagine a being next in order of perfection to God, lacking, say, only one perfection. For all we know the one lacking is the perfection of existence; thus the argument cannot be applied to anything less than God.

We can clarify much of this by pausing to make another point about logic. Arguments are constructed of propositions and traditional logic has thought of propositions as consisting of a subject term (S) and a predicate term (P) connected by a copula which is always some form of the verb "to be." The general form of the proposition in traditional logic is, then, "S is P," e.g. "Santa Claus is a fat man." "Santa Claus" is the subject term and "fat man" is the predicate term.

In some propositions the predicate term makes up part of the definition ("essence") of the subject. An example is when we define a triangle as a three-sided plane figure and then say that "triangles have three sides," that is, "three-sided figures have three sides." Such propositions are called *analytic* propositions because an "analysis," definition, of the subject term contains the predicate term. The general form of the analytic proposition is "ab is a" where "a" and "b" are the defining, essential, properties of the subject.

Descartes's argument for the existence of God really amounts to the contention that "God exists" is an analytic proposition. His definition of God as the completely perfect being amounts to the definition of God as that which possesses a, b, c, . . . n, n + 1, . . . where that indefinitely extended list is the list of all perfections. Since existence is supposedly a perfection in that list, let us say "n," then to say that God exists is to say that "the thing that is a, b, c, . . . n . . . is n." That is obviously analytic.

The standard objection to this version of the ontological argument comes from Immanual Kant's discussion of the ontological argument in his *Critique of Pure Reason*. The gist of this objection is that existence is not a predicate. Let us try to understand the point behind his objection. Predicate terms are descriptions of their subjects. They say what properties, characteristics, or features a thing is supposed to have. The point of describing something is often to distinguish it from other things. Suppose I tell you to go into the next cage and fetch my tiger. "Which one is yours?" is the obvious response. Let's imagine the exchange that follows. It's the one with stripes – but they all have stripes – it's the one with whiskers – but they all have whiskers – she's the one with the pink ribbon around her neck – ah, of course. Finally we got to the description that makes the necessary distinction. With the appropriate descriptive terms it is possible to sort out things. You can sort the tigers into the ones with stripes and the ones without, the ones with whiskers and the ones without, the ones with pink ribbons and the ones without.

The word "existence" does not work like a descriptive predicate. To say that something exists is not to describe the thing. Suppose in your position at the menagerie you are asked to put all the tigers with stripes into one cage and all the tigers whose stripes have faded in another. This you can do. Now you are asked to put all the ones that exist in here and all the others . . .? All the sense has been drained out of that order. At best it is a joke and the joke allows us to see that the word "exists" does not work at all like "has stripes."[9]

It is generally agreed these days that no proposition asserting the existence of anything can be an analytic proposition. To put it in a old-fashioned way, essence does not entail existence.

Analytic propositions are contrasted with synthetic propositions. Synthetic propositions assert that the subject has a property that is not part of its definition. "Triangles have three sides" is analytic, but "this triangle is scalene" is synthetic. Being scalene is not part of the definition of "triangle." Analytic propositions are necessarily true. They cannot be otherwise. This necessity, however, is gained at the expense of any factual content. To tell us that triangles have three sides is not to tell us anything about the facts of the world; at best it is to remind us of what the word means. Synthetic propositions, on the other hand, can give us information, but their truth is not necessary. They may be true and they may be false.

The ontological argument asserts that the existence of God is necessary. Although the argument itself rests upon confusion, there is nevertheless *something* right about the latter claim. We are inclined to say that nothing in the world exists necessarily. The desk at which I am sitting exists, but it might not have had I not gotten around to building it and one of these days it will cease to exist. You might not have existed had your parents never met and one of these days you will cease to exist. You and I and all the other furniture of the world have a history, that is, there was a time when we did not yet exist, certain things happened and here we are, and in the future other things will happen and we will pass like everything else.

Religious believers, however, cannot say that as a matter of fact there happens to be a God, but had things gone otherwise there might not have been. Nor can they say that God has a history. The Greek god Zeus had a history. He was the grandson of the original chief god, Ouranos, and, like his father Cronos before him, killed his father and then took over the job. We cannot ask how old God is or what he did when he was a little boy (little girl?). When children are told that God made the world, they sometimes want to know who made God. This is a question that cannot be asked, not because it is impious, but because it makes no sense. Having a history and all that goes with it is simply not part of our understanding of the concept of God. "You cannot ask how old God is" is rather like "you cannot score a goal in a tennis match." Talk about home runs in football makes no sense. Nonsense tends to result when we transfer the language that is appropriate to one area of activity and thought to another area where it has no application.[10] The ontological argument thus reminds us of something important about the *concept* of God, but cannot show us that there is such a God.

St Thomas Aquinas and the Cosmological Arguments

The changes that took place in Europe between the death of Anselm in the early twelfth century and the time of St Thomas Aquinas (1224/5–1274/5) were many and rapid. St Thomas' life spanned the middle of the thirteenth century and that is the century in which so many of the institutions and so much of the culture that we think of as characteristically medieval came to fruition. It was the century in which the power of the papacy reached its zenith before the so-called "Babylonian Captivity" of the papacy (1309–77) when the popes were resident in southern France and dominated by the French kings. It was the century in which the feudal organization of society reached its greatest development and the century in which the Gothic style of art and architecture which had its beginnings in the 1140s matured in the construction and completion of the great cathedrals at Chartres, Rheims, Notre-Dame and so many other places in France and England. What is especially important for our purposes, however, was the recovery by western scholars of the scientific and philosophical works of Aristotle that we spoke of in the last chapter.

It was the task of St Thomas Aquinas to undertake a reconciliation of Aristotle's science and the Christian religion, a reconciliation of faith and reason. St Thomas was a Dominican monk of Italian birth. He studied in various places in Italy, in Paris, and in Cologne. He also taught at several of those places. The intellectual life of the thirteenth century had become thoroughly international. The fact that Latin was the common language not only of the church but also of the new universities made it possible for scholars to travel anywhere in Christian Europe without the language barriers that we face today.

There were three assumptions behind the task of reconciling philosophy and religion: (1) by the use of reason Aristotle has provided the true scientific description of the world; (2) divine revelation has provided the true account of God and spiritual matters; and (3) reason and revelation are consistent with one another and reason can show that religious beliefs are rational.

In his *Summa Theologica* Thomas says that the existence of God can be proved in five ways. We shall examine in detail only the first and the fifth of these ways or arguments and simply mention the others. The first argument is the argument from motion and can be given this formulation.

> Something is in motion.
> Whatever is in motion is moved by another.
> The series of movers cannot be infinite.
> Therefore, there is a first mover and this everyone understands to be God.

The conclusion of the argument is that there must be a mover that moves other things, but is not itself moved, that is, is an unmoved mover.

The concept of motion at work in this argument is borrowed from Aristotle and the germ of the argument can be found in Books VII and VIII of Aristotle's *Physics*. For Aristotle and for Aquinas the word "motion" is used to describe several different kinds of changes although Aristotle does say that locomotion, movement from one place to another, is the primary kind of motion. For change or motion to take place a cause, a mover, must be acting. We can illustrate this idea by a couple of everyday examples. I set out to paint my house. My house is blue and I want to paint it white. As long as I wield the paintbrush the house is changing color from blue to white. As soon as I cease my labors the change stops. Now I want to move the sofa from one side of the living room to the other and I push and shove it into its new location. The sofa moves across the floor only so long as I push on it. I stop for a breather and the thing stops moving.

Aristotle describes the process of change as a passage from potentiality to actuality and Aquinas echoes this language. My house, which is actually blue, is potentially white, and the sofa, which is actually on this side of the room, is potentially on the other side. The change can be caused only by something that is actually in motion with respect to its object. Not everything is potentially just anything. While the sofa has the potentiality to be placed in many different positions, it does not have the potentiality to sprout wings and fly. An acorn has the potentiality to grow into an oak tree, but not into an apple tree. I am potentially a cause of change in the color of the house, the location of the sofa, and so on. The unmoved mover, however, is pure actuality and so requires nothing to cause its action.

Aristotle's argument to an unmoved mover takes place in the context of a theory of astronomy.[11] The earth is at the center of Aristotle's universe and is surrounded by a series of interconnected spheres to which are attached the moon, the sun, and the planets. The outermost sphere of all contains the fixed stars. The motion of this sphere causes the next inner sphere to turn which causes the next to revolve, and so on. It is the movements of the spheres of the sun and moon which cause seasonal changes to take place on earth. Without the changes of season life and everything else on earth would come to a halt. The unmoved mover must somehow stand outside the sphere of the fixed stars and keep it in eternal motion. If it ceased its activity, then everything else would cease.

Aristotle's argument and the Christianized version of it that Aquinas states is subject to a misunderstanding. When St Thomas speaks of a first mover he does not mean a cause that set the first thing in motion and then ceased to act. The picture that may be suggested is a series of dominoes stood on end. The first domino is knocked over and that one knocks over the next and so on down the line. The finger that gave the first push, however, no longer has anything to do. This is not the picture that either Aristotle or Thomas is offering us.

A better analogy is with a train of gears that mesh with one another. The turning of one gear causes the next to turn, which causes the rotation of the next, and so on. Let this train of gears be as long as we wish, even endless. What is required in this picture is something, or someone, that stands outside the series of gears to turn the crank to keep it all going. If the crank is not turned from the outside, the train of gears comes to an immediate halt. In like fashion the first and unmoved mover is required to keep the world going and not just to start it going.

Aristotle does not have a consistent account of how the first mover does its moving. In Book VII of the *Physics* he says that the causes of motion are pushing and pulling, but in the *Metaphysics*, Book XII, he says that the first mover moves by being an object of desire. It is by no means clear how this is to be understood but presumably we may suppose that the motion of the heavenly spheres is the result of their trying to imitate the perfect eternal motion of the unmoved mover. In the same book Aristotle entertains the possibility that there is a prime mover for each of the heavenly spheres and that there may be either 47 or 55 of them depending on how many spheres are necessary to explain the motions of the planets. St Thomas says nothing at all about how God, the first mover, does his moving.

However it is done, there is a fatal difficulty in the account. Let us imagine God turning a crank that makes the sphere of the fixed stars go round and that motion is in turn imparted to the inner spheres and so on to everything else in the world. If this is so, then God is continually putting energy into the world. But we cannot accept this conclusion. A fundamental principle of the natural sciences is the law of the conservation of energy that states that the amount of energy in the world is constant. All physics and chemistry presupposes this law. If the law did not hold, then it would be impossible to have these sciences. Since we do have these sciences and they are successful in describing and explaining natural phenomena, we must reject Aquinas' view of the matter.

We now have another interesting argument form to look at. The argument as just stated is this:

> If Thomas' argument for the existence of God is sound, then the law of the conservation of energy is false.
> The law is true, not false.
> Therefore, Thomas' argument is not sound.

Let us represent two distinct propositions by the letters "p" and "q" and we can then see that the argument is of the form:

> If p is true, then q is true.
> q is false.
> p is false.

This form of argument is used in the testing of theories and hypotheses. Any proper theory has consequences so that we can say that, if the theory is true, then we can expect certain other propositions to be true. Einstein's relativity theory, for example, predicted that light waves would be bent in a gravitational field. When the prediction was tested during a solar eclipse it proved to be true. That tended to confirm the theory. Had the prediction proved not true, the theory would have been shown to be false.[12]

It is not difficult to understand what has gone wrong in the Aristotelian/Thomistic theory of motion. That theory says that motion will take place only so long as a mover is acting. In the case of locomotion this suggests that a force must be pushing or pulling on a thing to keep it moving at constant speed, that is, that velocity is proportional to force.[13] This is not too far off when it is a matter of pushing a heavy sofa across the floor against a lot of friction, but it won't do as a general account of motion.

Modern mechanics tells us that a constant force does not produce a constant velocity, but rather a constant acceleration.[14] Acceleration is simply change in velocity. Velocity is a vector quantity and involves both rate of speed and direction of motion. Force is required to accelerate an object, that is, to change either its rate of speed or the direction in which it is moving. There is also a functional relation between velocity and energy so that energy is required to change the velocity of a moving object.[15] If the sphere of the fixed stars is eternally rotating, then its direction of motion is constantly changing and it is accelerating. This acceleration demands a constant input of energy that violates the law of energy conservation. It makes no difference whether we think of God as turning a crank to keep it all going or whether the motion arises in some different way. In either event an increasing quantity of energy that was not there before makes its appearance.

St Thomas' argument from motion is inextricably bound up with the physics and astronomy of his day that was inherited from Aristotle. It goes without saying that this science is mistaken and any view of God that is logically linked to it has to share in that mistake.[16] The argument can establish nothing for us.

There is, nevertheless, something important that the argument can call our attention to. The religious person is committed to the belief that in the beginning God created the heaven and the earth, but would have to deny the possibility that after creating it God stepped back and let everything go its own way.[17] God must be thought of as continually watching over and caring for His creation. In that respect the assumptions of the argument from motion are consistent with that view although believers need never have formulated their position at all theoretically.

The argument of the second way has the same structure as the first. The only difference is that Thomas substitutes the concept of an efficient cause for the concept of a mover. Since the order of efficient causes cannot proceed to infinity, there must be a first efficient cause and this is understood to be God. We may assume that the first efficient cause works just like the unmoved mover.

The third argument makes use of the notions of possibility and necessity. It is assumed that everything in the world could possibly not have existed. That is a way of saying that the existence of anything depends upon something else. If this is so, Aquinas says, then there would have been a time when nothing existed and he concludes that there must be a being whose existence is necessary, that is, depends upon nothing else, to explain the existence of the dependent world. He adds that this is what all men speak of when they speak of God. The argument also contains the premise familiar from the first two ways that any series of necessary beings cannot go on to infinity.

The premises assume that the world had to be created in time and that assumption cannot be accepted without considerable argument. The possibility that the world had no beginning cannot be ruled out ahead of time. We will talk about that in a later chapter. The notion of something whose existence is necessary is also a stumbling block. It is not at all clear how that is to be understood.

The fourth way is rather different from the first three and looks back more to a Platonic ancestry than an Aristotelian one. It is assumed that many of the characteristics things have are arranged in degrees. One thing can be hotter than another, for example, and that one hotter than some other, and so on. These degrees of more and less depend upon there being a maximum source of the quality in question, e.g. fire is said to be the maximum of heat and therefore the cause of degrees of heat in other things. There are also degrees of goodness and perfection in things and therefore this goodness and perfection must depend upon an ultimate cause of them which by now you have surely guessed is what we supposedly call God. The claim that degrees of a quality are caused by a maximum something is simply false. That fire is the maximum of heat and the cause of heat in other things is just bad physics.

The fifth way deserves attention because it contains a confusion that can trap us today and there is something to be learned by working through it. Thomas describes this way as taken from the governance of the world. It is sometimes called the teleological argument.[18] This is how it looks in our standard form.

> Things that lack intelligence, e.g. natural bodies, act for an end (purpose).
>
> Whatever lacks intelligence cannot act for an end unless directed by an intelligence.
>
> ---
>
> Therefore, there is an intelligent being by whom all natural things are directed to their end (God).

Note that the argument is not formally valid. There is nothing in the premises that entails that there is a *single* intelligence which directs the natural world. Let us not concentrate on that logical mistake, however, because it is the premises that deserve our attention.

There is every reason to believe that the second premise is true. It is only intelligent, i.e. conscious, beings such as people and some animals that have purposes and act to achieve them. Thomas' example of a natural body acting for a purpose is that of an arrow hitting a target. The arrow achieves the purpose of hitting the target, but only because it is directed by an archer. It is the purpose of the archer that the arrow should hit the target.

The justification for the first premise that natural bodies act for an end is the claim that they always, or nearly always, act in the same way. Thomas undoubtedly has in mind the movements of the stars and planets, the regular change of the seasons, the predictable behavior of the crops that sprout and grow, and the like. He is calling attention to the many regularities that the natural world exhibits and also no doubt to the many interconnections and interdependencies that are to be found in the natural world. These are the things that we would now subsume under the heading of laws of nature and also ecology.

The assumption behind this seems to be that regularity and organization denote purpose. We can be tempted to agree with this assumption by certain everyday considerations. Raise the hood of your car and gaze at the engine inside. Some engines have something called a carburetor. "What is that?" the uninitiated may ask. "What does it do; what is its purpose?" What it does (what its purpose is, what it was designed to do), of course, is to supply a proper mixture of fuel and air to be burned in the cylinders.

In addition to having a car, you also have a body. Were you to open it up you would see something called a heart and you may ask what it does, what its purpose is. As a matter of fact you scarcely have to ask because we all know that the heart pumps blood to the whole body and in doing so keeps you going. Now let us compare the question about the function of the carburetor in the ecology of the internal combustion engine with the question about the function of the heart in the ecology of the mammalian body.

The carburetor does something, plays a role, has a function, in the organization of the engine. It was also designed to do that. You can be taken to the factory to see the engineers at work on the design of the new and improved models. Here it makes sense to say that the carburetor achieves the purpose of the engineers. But, by contrast, when we learn that the function of the heart is to pump blood we cannot therefore conclude that that is its purpose, what it was designed to do. (Have you ever been to the engineering department?) When we are talking of machinery there is very little difference between talking of what a part does, what its function is, on the one hand and what its purpose is, what it was designed to do, on the other. Machinery, after all, is the product of intelligent design and in describing it we tend to collapse the notion of function into the notion of purpose.

We cannot do that, however, in the case of the things of nature. We can speak of the function of the various organs of the body, but we cannot speak of their purpose without begging the whole question at issue. To refer to the purpose of, say, the heart, is to imply that it was designed to carry out someone's purpose and that is the very thing that the argument seeks to establish. We must be careful in talking about natural things not to run the notion of function into the notion of purpose. The fact that there is regularity in the operations of nature and that living creatures have an organization is not sufficient to entail that any of it is the product of intelligence or design or purpose.

To be sure, early Greek science and philosophy had tended to describe nature in ways that we think of as appropriate only for people. Physical changes were sometimes to be explained in terms of justice, injustice, and retribution, and Aristotle made the notion of purpose important in his natural philosophy, although he thought of purposes – he called them final causes – as built into the nature of various things and not necessarily as the result of the guidance of some intelligent being. When the thinkers of the middle ages inherited Greek science and philosophy, especially that of Aristotle, it was all too easy for them as Christian thinkers to identify Aristotle's final causes with the purposes of God. Modern science, however, from its beginnings in the seventeenth century had to reject any reference to purposes or goals in order to get on with its mathematical theories of natural phenomena.[19]

St Thomas' arguments will not do. Even when they are formally valid they are part and parcel of a scientific view of the world that is simply mistaken; the arguments are not sound. If his arguments continue to hold a fascination for people, it may be because they are sometimes mistaken for another kind of argument that does have a decided appeal. It is to that argument that we now turn.

David Hume, the Dialogues Concerning Natural Religion, *and the Argument from Design*

David Hume (1711–76) was a native of Edinburgh, Scotland. Edinburgh was then the center of Scotch Presbyterianism. John Knox, the founder of that persuasion, had been a sixteenth-century resident of that city. Although

Hume had been brought up in the dominant religious atmosphere of Edinburgh, he rejected it and that alone was enough to ensure that he would never get the university post that he coveted. Hume wrote the *Dialogues* during the 1750s and made various revisions later, some shortly before his death. The work was not published, however, until 1779, three years after his death.

The title of the work refers to "natural religion," and that term merits a remark. Natural religion is to be contrasted with revealed religion. Traditionally it was assumed that religious belief is based on God having revealed Himself to men through scripture and the various prophets that He inspired, but it also came to be thought that we could arrive at knowledge of God and at religious belief by inference from the facts of the natural world which is taken to be the creation of God. It is the latter idea that Hume undertakes to examine in the *Dialogues*.

The *Dialogues* describe conversations between three participants, Demea, Cleanthes, and Philo. They are reported in the form of a letter from a young man, Pamphilus, to his friend, Hermippus. Pamphilus has been given over by his father to Cleanthes to supervise his education. It was while he was in the company of Cleanthes that he listened to the discussions between his tutor and his friends. We must grant that this is a rather slim literary device for getting across very important philosophical matters, but what is important is the philosophical reasoning and not the fragile literary framework.

Of special interest, however, is the description that Pamphilus gives of the three participants in the discussions. He speaks of the "accurate philosophical turn" of Cleanthes, the "careless scepticism" of Philo, and the "rigid inflexible orthodoxy" of Demea. It remains to be seen how accurate these characterizations really are.

In Part I of the *Dialogues* Cleanthes says that the order in which a student should learn philosophy is that recommended by the ancients, "first to learn logics, then ethics, next physics, last of all, of the nature of the Gods." Philo chides him for putting off teaching the principles of religion until last. Cleanthes replies by making an interesting distinction. He will teach piety and the practice of religion right from the beginning of a child's education; it is only religion as *science*, that is, as theory, philosophy, and theology, that will be postponed until the learner has acquired the necessary fundamental intellectual skills. This is not only an interesting, but an important distinction and we will bring out its importance in the last chapter.

Part II introduces the argument that is the subject of the balance of the *Dialogues*. Demea begins by claiming that there can be no question about the *existence* of God for the existence of God is self-evident; there can only be a question about the *nature* of God. The others agree that the question concerns the nature and not the existence of God although they do not agree on the matter of self-evidence. When he says that the existence of God is self-evident we must assume that he would accept some version of the ontological argument whereby the proposition "God exists" is understood to be analytic. He goes on to say that the nature of God must be altogether unknown and incomprehensible to us. Demea is here drawing the obvious conclusion that must follow from thinking of God as a completely transcendent being. If God is altogether transcendent, then He has no connection with the world that we live in and know; in that case, of course, we can't know anything about Him. God is not in any sense anthropomorphic, that is, like a human being. He cannot be said to have a physical body and, if he is pure spirit, then his spirit bears no relation to the human spirit or to human intelligence. Demea may have painted himself into a corner with this conception of an utterly transcendent God about which nothing can be said and, we should suspect, nothing at all can be known.

At this point Philo seems to agree with Demea that we cannot say anything about God. Our conceptions and the language in which we express them are designed for this world and have no application to that which is altogether transcendent. Philo argues for this conclusion by stating that our ideas reach no farther than our experience and that we have no experience of divine attributes and operations. He leaves readers to draw the conclusion from these premises for themselves. That conclusion is, if you have not already guessed it, that we have no ideas of the divine.

Arguments similar to this are advanced by Hume under his own name in other works. It marks him as an empiricist. Empiricism is the philosophical theory that all our knowledge is derived from sense experience. Hume couches all of this in terms of what he calls ideas. In the usage of seventeenth- and eighteenth-century British philosophy the word "idea" did duty for a number of things, sensations, perceptions, memories, feelings, emotions, thoughts, and conceptions. However they are to be understood, ideas are the stuff of knowledge and without the experience of our senses there can be no ideas and hence no knowledge.

It is here that Cleanthes states the argument we are to consider. To appreciate this argument we have to remind ourselves of the enormous changes in the world that took place in the five hundred years that divide David Hume from St Thomas Aquinas. There was the Italian Renaissance of the fifteenth century that began to push the art and culture of the middle ages off the stage and there was the Protestant Reformation of the sixteenth century that destroyed the religious unity of Europe for ever. But most important for now was the scientific revolution of the seventeenth century that changed completely the way we regard the physical world. That revolution began in the wake of Copernicus with the work of Kepler, Galileo, and Descartes in the first part of the century and came to fruition in the achievements of the incomparable Mr Newton in the latter part of the century. The result of Newton's work was what is sometimes spoken of as the mechanical view of the universe. Newton's mechanics and its remarkable success in explaining the behavior of projectiles and the movements of the planets made it seem plausible to many people that everything in the world could be explained in terms of mechanics. It is the mechanical view of the universe that stands behind Cleanthes' argument. Without the eighteenth century's familiarity with Newton the argument would have had little appeal.

The world, says Cleanthes, is a great machine subdivided into an infinite number of lesser machines. The most minute parts of these machines are adjusted to one another with an accuracy that "ravishes into admiration all men." This order and arrangement of things resembles the results of human contrivance. Since there is a resemblance in the effects, "we are led to infer, by all the rules of analogy, that the causes also resemble; and that the Author of nature is somewhat similar to the mind of man." He is careful to add that the Author of nature is far superior in intelligence and excellence to man.

The argument has this form:

The world is a complex machine.
As a machine the world is like man-made products.
Machines are the product of design and intelligence.

> The world machine is much more complex than any human product.
>
> ---
>
> The world must resemble human products in that it has an intelligent designer (God), but with far greater capacities than any human designer.

We must note two things about the argument. The first is that it really has two conclusions, (1) that there is an Author of nature and (2) that this Author or Great Designer has all the perfections that we wish to ascribe to God. The second is that it is an inductive argument rather than a deductive argument. As an inductive argument it has two aspects corresponding to the two conclusions: (1) Cleanthes tells us that the conclusion is inferred by "all the rules of analogy" and (2) it is an argument from effects to causes. He also characterizes it as an *a posteriori* argument.[20]

An argument from analogy reasons that, since two things are alike in some respects, there is a certain probability that they are alike in some other respect. Cleanthes says that the world machine is like a man-made machine and, since these machines have makers, the world probably has a maker.

We often reason from effects to causes. Robinson Crusoe came across footprints on what he had supposed was an Altogether Uninhabited Island and reasoned from the marks in the sand as effect to the fact that someone had walked there as cause. This kind of reasoning about causes can take another form. We can reason from the quality and complexity of a product to the skill and intelligence of its maker. The second part of Cleanthes' conclusion is the result of this sort of reasoning.

Demea immediately objects to this argument. The argument only makes it probable that God exists and

Demea's inflexibly rigid orthodoxy demands that God's existence be necessary and known *a priori*. We can sympathize with Demea at this point. No sincerely religious believer can be content with the claim that there probably is a God. The Christian Apostle's creed says, "I believe in God the Father Almighty, maker of heaven and earth . . .," not "I believe that there is a 93 percent probability that there is a God . . ." We do not pray "Our Father, if you really are in heaven, give us this day . . ." Cleanthes' argument clearly does violence to the whole spirit of religion.

The argument, nevertheless, is appealing to a great many people. It is a version of the second line of reasoning that we examined in the section on "Reasons for Believing that God Exists" earlier in this chapter. While the starry heavens above may seem to these people to demand a Creator, more than likely they have not thought through the traps that can lurk in causal reasoning. Philo does us the service of teaching us about some of these.

Philo sets aside Demea's objection that probability is out of place with respect to God and goes after the argument itself. The argument, he says in effect, is not even a good inductive or analogical argument. Before looking at what Philo says in criticism let's do our own thinking about arguments of this kind.

Suppose your car is not running well; the engine is making an odd noise and there is little acceleration. You take the car to the garage and explain the symptoms to the mechanic. He notes the year, make, and model of your car and the kind of engine it has. He says that in his experience when cars like yours make that kind of noise the problem is usually a flaw in the timing gear and that is probably the trouble with your car. He then proceeds to check the timing gear to verify his hypothesis.

What allows him to draw that probable conclusion? He has repaired any number of cars of that make, model, and engine type and in a large percentage of cases has found that the offending noise is caused by a faulty timing gear. This creates a high probability that it is your trouble also. The greater his experience with cars of that sort, the greater will be his confidence in his diagnosis. Had he seen only one or two other cars he would not have had much to go on. The number of *relevant* similarities between your car and the others is also important. Year, make, model, and engine type are obviously relevant, but if he bases his diagnoses on the color of the car and the name of the salesman from whom you bought it you would be well advised to take your trade to another garage.

Note also that his conclusion that it is probably a flaw in the timing gear is really an hypothesis that remains to be confirmed. His reasoning does not guarantee that it is the timing gear. His hypothesis may be confirmed and again it may not, but it gives him a good place to start work; he will check the timing gear first.

Philo points out that when we see a house we can be assured that it had an architect or builder. This is because we have seen houses being built and we know how they come to be. The next house we see is sufficiently like the others so there can be no doubt that it also had a builder. He adds that the universe is not so similar to a house that we can infer that it also has a builder. Cleanthes counters that the adjustment of means to ends in the world is very much like that in a house; just as stairs are designed for climbing so are legs designed for walking.

Philo now has recourse to his empiricist principles. Our knowledge of causes and their effects is based on our experience. Imagine someone put into the world, like Adam we may suppose, without any previous experience of anything. Such a one would not know that fire burns or that a daily apple will keep the doctor away. It requires experience to learn that this causes that and eventually that similar effects are the result of similar causes. The gist of Philo's criticism of the argument can be put very simply. We have no experience of worlds being designed and built as we have of houses and other human artifacts. We cannot then reason, "Here is a world, therefore Somebody designed and built it," as we can when we see a house and conclude that it was designed and built. The question is thus not merely about the nature of God as was stated earlier, but very much about His existence.

Philo agrees with Cleanthes that intelligence is a cause of design and order, but qualifies this agreement by reminding us that our experience of intelligence involves only human intelligence and its resulting human activity and this is apparently limited to a tiny corner of a vast universe. This is obviously insufficient inductive evidence for reaching any conclusion at all about the role of intelligence in the universe as a whole.

There is another thing about Cleanthes' argument that must be noted although Philo says nothing about it. The best that this species of argument can give us is a more or less probable hypothesis as in the case of the garage mechanic. The hypothesis remains to be confirmed. In the case of God there doesn't seem to be any independent way of confirming the hypothesis generated by the argument. It is indeed an odd inductive argument whose conclusion is incapable of confirmation.

Cleanthes' argument is not sufficient to reach his first conclusion that there is an Author of nature, a Someone or Something that created the world, or even to make it the least bit probable; in fact, it cannot even get off the ground. If this is so, then it would seem that the second part of Cleanthes' conclusion about the excellence and perfection of this originating cause can simply be set aside as having no application to anything. Philo, however, is not going to let it stand at that. He wants to complete the wrecking job that he has begun. His strategy is to allow, for the sake of wrapping it all up, that the argument from design does establish that there is an originating cause of the world. He will then show that this conclusion can by no means guarantee that this cause is anything like the God of traditional theism.

Both Cleanthes and Philo grant that we often reason from effects to causes. A special case of this kind of reasoning occurs in relation to human activity when we reason from the quality of a piece of work to the quality of the workman. A craftsman is known by the quality of his work. We admire a custom-made piece of furniture and remark that the cabinet maker who built it must have been a master craftsman. Can we do the same with respect to the world? Can we say that this is a most excellent world and thus must have had a most excellent Maker?

In order to judge the quality of any human product we must have some criteria or standards. These standards are acquired by experience. To judge that this is a well-made piece of furniture we must have at least some experience of what can be done with wood and tools. The work that we admire in the beginning may appear to us rather crude later in our careers when we have had a chance to know more about the possibilities of human skill.

Philo gives us his example of this sort of thing in Part V when he asks whether a peasant could judge the merit of the *Aeneid*[21] if it were read to him. The "peasant" is, of course, chosen as an example of someone who is not only illiterate, but also knows nothing of poetry. To judge the merit of a poem, or any work of art for that matter, you must know a good bit about what can be done with artistic materials.

Let's apply what we have just reminded ourselves of to the world. Is this an excellent world? To answer this question the first thing we must do is to ask what standards and criteria are to be used. What are the marks of a good world? Is this one a better job of work than that other one? What are the possibilities for working with world-making materials? It ought to be obvious that there are no answers to these questions and that we have no idea of what it is to judge the merits of a world as we can judge the merits of human artifacts.

Suppose someone says that the fact that the earth is fit for human habitation shows that this is a good world. We have to ask this person what relevance this fact has for the value of the entire world. Is the fact that this little planet revolving around one small star out of countless billions supports a certain kind of life a mark of excellence? We have no way of knowing. The attempt to infer the excellence of the world Maker from the excellence of the world breaks down completely.

In Part V Philo goes on to spell out more disturbing consequences of Cleanthes' argument. A shipbuilder, for example, may be only a "stupid mechanic" who learned his trade by trial and error. The greater part of human artifacts are not created by a single craftsman, but by the cooperation of any number of people; think of the way automobiles are manufactured. Cleanthes can be thought of as offering a better argument for polytheism than for monotheism. Since we have no way to judge the quality of the world for all we know the world may be the product of an apprentice God, "the first rude essay of some infant Deity," or of some senile God whose hand shook in the process.

Philo charges that Cleanthes' position commits him to anthropomorphism, the thesis that God or the gods are like human beings. This position does not rule out the possibility that there are many gods, that they have varying levels of skill, and even that they have human physical characteristics and procreate like us. That takes us right back to the gods of the Greeks and is altogether inconsistent with the conception of God common to Judaism and Christianity.

Philo has managed to pull off as thorough a job of philosophical demolition as we are likely to find. There is nothing left of Cleanthes' argument from design when he has done with it. It is, therefore, disheartening to find one or another version of the argument still being appealed to by religious people. Such people are cutting off the very limb they want to sit on. We will return to that difficulty later.

There are, however, a couple of points in the*Dialogues* still to be mentioned. In Part III Cleanthes says in response to Philo's criticism, "Consider, anatomize the eye: survey its structure and contrivance; and tell me, from your own feeling, if the idea of a contriver does not immediately flow in upon you with a force like that of a sensation." Philo has made clear that the assumption of contrivance in such cases will not stand intellectual scrutiny, but suppose we understand Cleanthes to be doing something other than asserting a proposition to serve as a premise in an argument and to be judged as either true or false. He does, after all, speak of a *feeling*, we might say, of a *reaction* that a person can have to the world. It may be that such reactions can play an important role in religious life. Let us note this as one more loose end to be tied up in the last chapter.

There is a strong temptation to suppose that the character of Philo speaks for Hume himself for he does make use of the same empiricist principles that Hume advocates under his own name. It is therefore surprising to find Philo apparently agreeing with Cleanthes that "the cause or causes of order in the universe probably bear some remote analogy to human intelligence." On closer inspection, however, the agreement is more apparent than real; these causes are incomprehensible to us and Philo claims this has no relevance to human life and refuses to draw from it any of the conclusions about God and the world that Cleanthes is after.

After all the returns are in from the *Dialogues* it seems clear that Cleanthes' philosophical turn was not nearly as precise as Pamphilus would have it nor Philo's skepticism nearly so careless. Pamphilus, however, is allowed to conclude that he thinks Cleanthes has got the better of the discussion.

Preliminary Conclusions

We have now examined several traditional arguments for the existence of God and found them all wanting. There is, however, an additional argument referred to as the moral argument, but we will postpone discussion of that until we come to deal with the relation between religion and ethics in chapter 5. Anselm's ontological argument can be stated in a way that is formally valid, but because of its false premises is unsound. St Thomas' unmoved mover argument is also formally valid although unsound. His teleological argument is invalid and one of its premises is false in the bargain. Cleanthes' argument from design is an inductive argument and a worthless one of that kind.

We might be tempted to conclude from this that the existence of God cannot be proved, but that would be a hasty generalization. The fact that the arguments examined so far fail does not entail that every future argument must fail. Perhaps we have just not come upon the right one yet. There is, however, a consideration that must cast doubt on the whole procedure of arguing for the existence of God.

It is a fact about deductive arguments that you cannot get a reference to anything in the conclusion that is not already mentioned in one of the premises. Consider the hoary logic text example:

All men are mortal.
Socrates is a man.
Therefore, Socrates is mortal.

The conclusion refers to both Socrates and being mortal and these two are also referred to in the premises. Suppose, however, that instead of the conclusion that Socrates is a man we conclude that Socrates is a taxidermist. Since there is no mention of taxidermists in the premises, the conclusion is illegitimate and the argument invalid.

The moral of this example and the logical principle it illustrates is that, if we wish to construct a deductive argument to the conclusion that God exists, then at least one of the premises must be a proposition about God. It is more than doubtful that we can introduce a proposition about God into the premises without begging the very question at issue. There would be insuperable questions about how we know such a proposition is true.

As for inductive arguments, Hume, in the person of Philo, has shown that they all rest on our experience of the facts of the world and therefore cannot take us to God who must be thought of as something apart from the world.

Perhaps it would not be wise to deny categorically that there can be a sound argument for the existence of God, but it is the part of wisdom to admit a strong presumption against the possibility. There are people who will occasionally take this to be an attack on religion as if pointing out the failure of the various arguments amounts to denying the existence of God. That is a serious logical mistake. That an argument is unsound, whether it is formally invalid or its premises false, tells us nothing about the truth or falsity of its conclusion. Invalid and unsound arguments can have true conclusions. If the various arguments fail, all that we are entitled to conclude is simply that you can't get to God that way, not that there is no God to get to. It may be the case that arguments are irrelevant to religion, and that suggestion is another loose end to be tied up later.

Suggestions for Further Reading

The nature of argument

The number of introductory logic texts is legion and most of them will do an adequate job of explaining what an argument is and what some of the elementary principles of logic are. The best of the lot is probably James D. Carney and Richard K. Scheer, *Fundamentals of Logic* (New York: Macmillan, 1964).

St Anselm

Alvin Plantinga, ed., *The Ontological Argument: From St Anselm to Contemporary Philosophers* (Garden City, NY: Doubleday Anchor Books, 1965), is a useful anthology of the major classical and contemporary versions and criticisms of the argument. See also his *The Nature of Necessity* (Oxford: Clarendon Press, 1974), chap. X, for a sophisticated discussion of the argument and recent versions of it from the point of view of modern logical developments.

St Thomas Aquinas

For a lucid account of Aristotle's physical and metaphysical views that underlie the arguments of St Thomas see W. D. Ross, *Aristotle*, 5th edn (London: Methuen & Co., 1956). F. C. Copleston, *Aquinas* (Harmondsworth, Middlesex: Penguin Books, 1955), is a helpful introduction to the thought of St Thomas. G. E. M. Anscombe and P. T. Geach, *Three Philosophers* (Ithaca: Cornell University Press, 1961), has good discussions of both Aristotle and Aquinas. Anthony Kenny, *The Five Ways* (New York: Schocken Books, 1969), is a detailed examination of each of Thomas' arguments. Donald B. Burrill, ed., *The Cosmological Arguments: A Spectrum of Opinion* (Garden City, NY: Doubleday Anchor Books, 1967), is an interesting collection of classical and recent work concerning that kind of argument.

David Hume

The best edition of Hume's *Dialogues Concerning Natural Religion* is that of Norman Kemp Smith (New York: Macmillan, Library of Liberal Arts, 1988). Kemp Smith's introductory essays about and analyses of the *Dialogues* are invaluable. A good general introduction to Hume's thought is A. H. Basson, *David Hume* (Harmondworth, Middlesex: Penguin Books, 1958). Not to be missed is Ernest C. Mosner's biography, *The Life of David Hume* (Oxford: Clarendon Press, 1970).

Notes

1. We can speak not only of empirical *questions* but also of empirical *statements*. An empirical statement is one whose truth or falsity must be determined by empirical observation.
2. There is a technical distinction between deduction and entailment, but that belongs to a serious course in logic.
3. It is often useful to test an argument by comparing it with another that has the same structure. Do you believe what you read in the headlines of the grocery store tabloids, e.g. "Farmer shoots 6 foot butterfly"?
4. Logicians call this form *modus ponens*. It is one of the most commonly used argument forms.
5. The German philosopher Immanuel Kant gave the name to this species of argument in his *Critique of Pure Reason*, first published in 1781.
6. This word is derived from the Greek word *theos* meaning "god" together with the Greek negative prefix "*a*". The *theist*, then, is one who believes there is a God and the *a-theist* is one who denies there is a God.
7. See Anselm's *Dialogue on Truth* in Richard McKeon, ed., *Selections from Medieval Philosophers*, vol. 1 (New York: Charles Scribner's Sons, 1929).
8. The argument is found in *Meditation* V.
9. Modern formal logic symbolizes reference to existence in quite different ways than it does genuine predicates. The proposition "Tigers exist" is construed, roughly, as equivalent to saying that there is a least one way of filling in the blank that makes the sentence form "____ is a tiger" into a true proposition.
10. Note the similarity of the philosophical move made here to the one made in chapter 1 where it was pointed out that it makes no sense to ask about the physical characteristics of a transcendent God.
11. The details of this are developed in Aristotle's *On the Heavens*.

12 This rather oversimplifies the complexity of scientific and experimental procedures. It would have to be ascertained that the data had been correctly recorded, that the experimental apparatus was functioning properly, that there were no disturbing influences, and the like. For all that, the principle of the argument is still at work.

13 Aristotle never put it this way. He never provided a mathematical representation of motion; that had to wait until the seventeenth century. This is our way of representing it and it will help us to realize the shortcoming of Aristotelian science.

14 Newton's second law of motion states that force = mass × acceleration, $F = ma$.

15 Energy = mass × velocity^2, i.e. $E = mv^2$.

16 To say that Greek science was mistaken is not to say that it was foolish or that the Greeks were blind to the true facts about the solar system. Without the Greek and medieval preliminaries and the problems they wrestled with modern science would have been unthinkable.

17 Such a view gained considerable popularity during the eighteenth century under the name of *deism*. Its popularity tended to be restricted to philosophers and other intellectuals. It is altogether at odds with the traditions of Judaism and Christianity. Alexander Pope's *An Essay on Man* (1733–4) is a poetic expression of deistic ideas.

18 "Teleological" is from the Greek word *telos* which refers to goals, purposes, and aims.

19 Some have argued that teleological explanations may be necessary to account for certain biological phenomena, but these modern theoretical speculations have nothing to do with anything Aquinas was speaking of.

20 The term *a posteriori* and its companion *a priori* indicate after and before experience. *A priori* propositions are those that can be known to be true before or, better, independently of experience, that is, without looking to see what things are like. Analytic propositions are known to be true without

having to check the facts. The truth of *a posteriori* propositions, by contrast, can only be determined by investigating the facts of the world. The truth of the proposition "the door is open" must be determined by looking to see how things are with the door.

21 The great epic poem of Virgil, written in the first century BC, recounting the legendary founding of Rome by the Trojan prince, Aeneas.

3

The Bible, Truth, and History

Biblical Inerrancy

In the last chapter we saw that one of the reasons that people sometimes give for believing that God exists is the testimony of the Bible. To use the testimony of the Bible as a premise in an argument for the existence of God is, as we also saw, hopelessly circular. The argument depends upon the assumption that what the Bible says is true and the justification for that assumption is that the Bible is the word of God. The Bible does occupy a central place in both Judaism and Christianity and, whether or not circular reasoning is involved, many people will claim that their religious faith does rest upon the Bible. It is of vital importance to many religious people to believe that the Bible is true. Our task in this chapter, therefore, is to investigate the question: Is the Bible true?

As students of philosophy let us consider that task. To investigate the question is not the same as to answer the question. The answer to the question Is the Bible true? would appear to be either "yes" or "no"; or, more carefully, "these statements are true, but these others are not." To investigate the *question*, however, is to ask questions about the question. We will have to ask what kind of question we are considering, that is, what sort of investigation is appropriate to answering it. We must ask, for example, questions such as: To what extent are historical and archeological findings relevant? Can the truth of the statements in the Bible be established by the methods of empirical science? Is everything that is of importance in the Bible expressed in *propositions*? After all, it is only propositions that can be either true or false. Are all the statements in the Bible consistent with one another? Two propositions that are inconsistent cannot both be true. If two propositions in the Bible are inconsistent, which one of them is true and how do we tell? And then, of course, we will eventually have to ask what the implications for religion and the religious life are should the Bible prove to be true or prove, at least in part, to be false.

There is a form of the belief that the Bible is true that is known as the doctrine of Biblical inerrancy. The doctrine states that the Bible is inerrant, that is, true, in everything it says, not only about God, but also about history and science. This doctrine is associated with the movement within conservative evangelical protestantism known as fundamentalism. There has been a tendency in the last few years to use the word "fundamentalism" to characterize almost any kind of conservative religious movement and this has led many to speak of Catholic fundamentalism and even Islamic fundamentalism. We shall, however, confine our use of the term to its original application to American Protestantism. Since Protestant fundamentalism has been a force in both religion and politics in recent years, especially in the United States, it will be helpful to say a word about that movement.

The name "fundamentalism" comes from a series of pamphlets published between 1910 and 1915 with the title *The Fundamentals*. These publications were the idea of a wealthy Los Angeles businessman, Lyman Stewart, who paid for the project. The tracts were written by a number of prominent conservative evangelical theologians and widely distributed to church groups. *The Fundamentals* focused attention on a kind of religious position that had been several decades in the making.

By the beginning of the nineteenth century a number of scientific and intellectual developments were proving very uncongenial to traditional Protestantism. For one thing, geology was being put on a proper scientific basis and careful observation of the earth and its natural processes were making clear to geologists that the earth was much older than most people had believed it to be. In the seventeenth century James Ussher (1581–1656), an Irish bishop and scholar, had calculated on the basis of the various genealogies in the Bible that the world was created in 4004 BC.[1] Ussher's date was widely accepted. The observation of the processes of erosion and the like, however, made it obvious that the earth, not to mention the whole universe, was incalculably older than anyone had supposed.

This was also a time when Biblical scholarship was making a great deal of progress and many traditional notions about the age and authorship of the scriptures were being challenged. And then, of course, in 1859 Charles Darwin published his *Origin of Species* which, it was widely assumed, challenged the Biblical account of creation and the unique status of man.

These developments were very disturbing to many traditional Protestants. Although some denominations began to try to make their peace with the new science and scholarship, many did not. These new ideas were lumped together under the disparaging title of "modernism" and in the latter part of the nineteenth century various church organizations undertook to defend their traditional positions against the encroachments of what they took to be the dangerous tide of modernism. The publication of *The Fundamentals* must be understood as an episode in the fight to preserve a certain species of traditional Protestantism. The doctrine of Biblical inerrancy was a point insisted upon in those tracts.

Both Judaism and Christianity had traditionally accepted scripture as in some sense authoritative. Protestantism especially emphasized the importance of scripture. During the Reformation it had argued that the church rests upon scripture and that Roman Catholicism had strayed from scriptural teaching and thus corrupted true Christianity. Fundamentalism's view of Biblical inerrancy, whatever it owes to the Reformation stance, is more immediately the result of doctrines worked out at Princeton Theological Seminary, a Presbyterian institution, during the first half of the nineteenth century and more or less fully formulated by 1850.

Fundamentalism is frequently accused of being anti-intellectual although this is not true of its nineteenth-century evangelical roots. It based itself on a very respectable philosophical tradition. This tradition was a combination of the philosophy of science of Sir Francis Bacon (1561–1626) and the philosophy known as Scottish Common Sense Realism of Thomas Reid (1710–96). Reid objected to the philosophical conclusions of the British philosophical tradition developed by John Locke, George

Berkeley, and David Hume. Without going into the details, this philosophy tended to end in skepticism, the philosophical theory that we cannot have any knowledge at all about the world. Since the only things we are said to be actually aware of are our own sense impressions, we can never know whether there is a world of objects that exists independently of our minds or whether there is any truth to be gotten about anything. Reid claimed that this conclusion ran up against the common sense of mankind that teaches us that there is a world out there that we are all directly aware of. If the theories of the philosophers run afoul of common sense, then those theories must give way to the common understanding of human beings. Not only did Reid disagree with his contemporary countryman, David Hume, about the nature of knowledge, but he also disagreed with him in accepting traditional religious beliefs and in having no doubt that the world displayed clear evidence of design.[2]

In addition to unquestioned acceptance of traditional religious beliefs the religious movement that was to become fundamentalism picked out several features of this Scottish philosophy of common sense that were to become especially important in its development. For our purposes it will be useful to focus on three of these.

The first was the apparently democratic emphasis on the ability of individuals to decide matters of truth for themselves. You do not need to be a philosopher or an educated scholar to distinguish the true from the false; the common people can be their own arbiters of truth. This was taken to apply both to discovering the facts of the natural world by reading the book of nature and to discovering the word of God by reading the Bible. The Princeton theologian, Charles Hodge, made this point very clear when he said in 1855 that "The Bible is a plain book. It is intelligible by the people. And they have the right and are bound to read and interpret it for themselves; so that their faith may rest on the testimony of the Scriptures, and not that of the Church."[3] And then he would go on to say (in 1871) that "The Bible is to the theologian what nature is to the man. It is his store-house of facts . . ."[4] The authors of the scriptures were thought to be simply reporting the facts they were presented with.

The second feature we will note was a general distrust of theory. Truth lies in the facts themselves and the facts of the world are open to all to observe. Theory was taken to be unverified speculation that went beyond anything that was justified by facts. This distrust of theory applied not only to the theories of philosophers that supposedly went against the grain of common sense, but also to what we would think of as scientific theories. In the first half of the nineteenth century, we might note, there was no hard and fast distinction between philosophy and science. In his view of science Thomas Reid was very much a follower of Sir Francis Bacon. Bacon lived at the time the scientific revolution of the seventeenth century was just getting under way and he is often thought of as an early proponent of the scientific method. He outlined the method that he believed that scientific investigation should follow. Science should proceed by the careful observation of nature. It should be essentially the compilation, organization, and comparison of natural phenomena together with what can be deduced from these facts of experience. Expressed rather crudely in modern terms, the method tells us to collect as many facts as possible and then perform statistical analyses on them in order to reveal the laws and principles of nature. Both Bacon and Reid were opposed to theory for they tended to think of theory in terms of the philosophical speculations of the Greek and medieval philosophers which too often had no connection to the actual facts of the world.

Bacon himself made no contributions to science and the method he advocated was not the method that was actually used by the pioneers of modern science. Isaac Newton could never have arrived at his laws of motion by compiling and arranging the observed facts of motion. The law of inertia states that a body in motion that is not acted upon by any force will continue in motion in the same straight line. No one, needless to say, has ever observed anything moving free of all forces in a straight line eternally. This law could never have been deduced from any facts about the movement of objects. The formulation of the law required an act of imagination that went far beyond the observation of any actual phenomenon. Newton's laws, however, permit us to understand and explain the actual facts of motion.

Finally there were the implications to be drawn from the emphasis upon scripture as the *word* of God. The *word* of God was understood to be manifested in *statements*. If scripture is inerrant and infallible, it is because it states true propositions. Fundamentalism tends to see the essence of religion as the belief that certain *propositions* are true. Other aspects of religion such as religious experience, traditions, and rituals take a back seat to beliefs. Experience, traditions, and rituals can all change, but the word of God endures for ever. Like diamonds, true propositions are for ever.

With this background in mind let us go on to examine the doctrine of Biblical inerrancy itself. We will look at a recent presentation of the doctrine by Gleason L. Archer in his widely available book, *Encyclopedia of Biblical Difficulties*.[5] Archer follows the nineteenth-century tradition in telling us that the doctrine is crucially important because unless the Bible is inerrant in all things, including scientific and historical matters, then it cannot be trusted in theological matters either. An opening for doubt about any particular matter opens the way for general doubt about the truth of the scriptures as a whole. Christians must take their stand upon scripture and can admit no question about it.

It may be helpful to point out before we go on that doctrine of Biblical inerrancy need not entail that the Bible must be read as literally true. In many places the fundamentalist is quite willing to interpret scripture as metaphor or allegory. A characteristic example is a common treatment of the Song of Songs (Song of Solomon). In that work we read "Your breasts are like two fawns, / Twins of a gazelle, / Browsing among the lilies" (4:5). Read literally the work is love poetry in praise of the beloved's various assets. It has been a Christian tradition, however, to interpret the work as an allegory of Christ's love for His church. Some Bibles gloss each chapter in this way.

Archer presents an argument[6] for Biblical inerrancy that goes like this:

> The Christian accepts Christ as the supreme authority.
> Whatever Christ believed about the authority of scripture must be true.
> Christ accepted the scriptures as factual.
> Therefore, the scriptures are true, i.e. the Bible is inerrant.

The argument is question-begging, but not quite in the same way that some other arguments are. The grounds for supposing that Jesus is indeed the Christ and therefore the supreme authority are not what is said throughout the Bible generally, but are the claims about Jesus presumably made in the gospels and made explicitly in other New

Testament writings. The argument says in effect that, if the New Testament claims about Jesus as the Christ are true, then everything else in the Bible is true and inerrant. One must, therefore, assume that the New Testament is true in order to argue that the rest of the Bible is true. The New Testament is being asked to certify its own truth. Very little logical sophistication is needed to recognize that such an argument is hopeless.

There are, however, interesting issues in some of the details that we are offered in support of the third premise in the argument. Archer mentions several instances in which Jesus cited scripture. In Matthew 12:40, for example, Jesus says that "For as Jonah was three days and three nights in the belly of a huge fish, so the Son of Man will be three days and three nights in the heart of the earth." This is taken to show that Jesus believed that the story of Jonah and the fish was true. And, as the argument has it, if Jesus believed it was true, then it must be true. There are several problems in this line of argument.

In the first place we don't really know what Jesus said. Although the evangelical Christian has no doubt that the gospels present a true account of the life and teaching of Jesus, this is not true of others. As a matter of fact there is no general agreement among serious Biblical scholars about which sayings in the gospels report the actual words of Jesus and which are attributed to him by various traditions. We will return to this point later. In the second place, assuming the words are those of Jesus, the fact that he makes reference to a number of scriptural passages does nothing to establish that the entire Bible is inerrant. All the books that now compose the Hebrew Bible were in circulation when Jesus lived, but they had not been collected into a single volume called The Bible. The official canon of the Hebrew Bible was not fixed until the last decade of the first century AD and then it was a matter of selecting and excluding from a number of works. We do not know how much of that collection Jesus knew nor what non-canonical books he may have known and endorsed. The argument from Jesus' references cannot, of course, be used to conclude anything about the inerrancy of the New Testament books which did not come into existence until well after Jesus' death.

There is a further problem in the argument. The fact that someone cites a story to make a point does not necessarily entail that the person believes the story is true. Suppose you have a friend who is getting on in years and who mentions that he is thinking of dividing his worldly goods among his children. He then plans to sell his house and to live part of the year with each of his children in turn. You are well aware that this may not be a wise course of action, that children can be ungrateful, and that a thankless child can be sharper than a serpent's tooth. To alert your friend to this danger you remind him about King Lear. I assume that you do not believe for a moment that Shakespeare's tale of King Lear is true. The allusion to the play, however, is an excellent way to make your point. In like manner, the fact that Jesus cites Jonah by way of analogy with his own situation does not demand that we believe Jesus thought the story to be true. Perhaps he did, but he certainly need not have in order to make effective use of the story.

Whoever supports the doctrine of Biblical inerrancy has any number of serious problems to contend with. Let us note two kinds of these. The first five books of the Hebrew Bible, what Christians call the Pentateuch (which is Greek for "the five scrolls") and Jews call Torah (Teaching), contain any number of apparent inconsistencies.[7] In the account of creation in the first chapter of

Genesis man, both male and female, is the last of all things to have been created. In the second chapter man, Adam, the male only, is created before there is vegetation and animals. Archer's strategy in cases such as this is to deny that there is any inconsistency and to explain away the appearance of any inconsistency. With reference to Adam's case he says that the account in Genesis 1 gives the order of events and Genesis 2 simply concentrates attention on man.[8] For the time being we can pass over the fact that this tactic gets by only by ignoring the rest of the text.

The other type of problem lies in trying to make sense of the various extraordinary and miraculous events reported in scripture that strain our capacity to believe. As a case in point let us take Archer's treatment of the story of the sun standing still for Joshua.[9] The account is found in Joshua 10. Joshua, who was the war leader of the Israelites in their invasion of Canaan, was engaged in battle against a people called the Amorites. He had routed the Amorite army and inflicted heavy losses upon them. We may assume that it was getting dark and there would soon not be enough light to continue the slaughter. In the presence of the Israelites Joshua called upon the Lord: " 'Stand still, O sun, at Gibeon, / O moon in the valley of Aijalon!" . . . Thus the sun halted in midheaven, and did not press on to set, for a whole day." How are we to understand this supposed phenomenon of the sun standing still?

As we have already seen, the ancient Israelites did not have science and consequently did not have any theory about the nature of the heavenly bodies and their movements. We look in vain for any systematic account of the relation between the earth and the heavens. They did, however, apparently believe that the earth was flat and that the heavens made a dome over the earth. Imagine that you are standing in a large hall covered by a dome. There is a track that runs across the dome from one side to the other and there is a light attached to it so it can move across the dome on the track. Perhaps it is run by a motor or there is a chap who pulls it across with a rope. At any point in its motion across the dome it would possible to command that the light stop moving; the person in charge turns off the motor or stops pulling the rope and the light stands still. This is no doubt the way in which the Israelites thought about the sun. God makes it move across the dome of the sky every day and there would be nothing at all out of order in imagining Him to stop its motion whenever it suited Him.

But this is not how things are. What appears to us as the sun moving across the sky is actually the result of the earth turning upon its own axis. In order for the sun to stand still to permit Joshua to kill more Amorites the earth would have to stop rotating. We must think about the consequences of that. The circumference of the earth at the equator is only slightly less than 25,000 miles. The earth rotates once every 24 hours. This means that any object at the equator has a linear velocity of more than 1,000 miles an hour. It the earth were suddenly to stop rotating the law of inertia tells us that anything not securely tied down would continue to move in a straight line tangent to the surface of the earth at its original velocity of 1,000 miles an hour. If this happened there would still be bunny rabbits and toad frogs in orbit, not to mention cataclysmic geological disruptions of the earth's surface. The enormous inertial forces generated by such a sudden halt would have destroyed everything on the planet if not the earth itself.

Since there are no such curious objects flying around in space and no evidence of any such geological disturbances, we can only conclude that the earth did not stop rotating.

The form this argument takes should already be familiar to us:

> If the earth stopped rotating, then there would be such and such evidence.
> There is no such evidence.
> Therefore, the earth did not stop rotating.

Or schematically:

> If p, then q.
> Not q.
> Not p.

One would be inclined to think that this objection settles the issue and shows without doubt that the story of Joshua is not only false, but that anyone who believes it must be hopelessly ignorant of physics. There is, however, a response to it from the Biblical inerrantist.

Archer makes two principal moves in rebuttal. One is to read the phrase "the sun . . . did not press on to set, for a whole day" to mean that the sun did not stop, but only slowed down so that the day was 48 instead of 24 hours long. It would be an interesting exercise to calculate what inertial forces would be generated by an immediate 50 percent reduction in the speed of the earth's rotation. We know what happens to the passengers in a car going 60 miles an hour that comes to a sudden halt. Think of what also happens if it were suddenly to slow to 30 miles an hour. For the earth's rotation to slow so that the inertial effect is minimized or unnoticed would require quite an extended period of time.

Archer's other move is really much more interesting. God is omnipotent and has the infinite power to stop the rotation of the earth and at the same time to hold all the laws of physics in abeyance. God could have stopped the earth and left everything else unchanged. This move allows us to focus attention on something very important about the way we seek to understand the world we live in. We tend to conduct our affairs in the confidence that the way things are now is evidence for the way they used to be. This is the case not only in science, but also in our day-to-day affairs. The dirty dishes in the sink tell me that someone failed to wash them last night. The footprints in the flower bed make clear that the burglar came in through that window. The signature and date on the contract guarantee that the business deal has been made. The marine fossils found on these hills are evidence that this was once sea bottom. If God could have stopped the earth's rotation and left everything else the same, then the way things are now is not evidence for what happened in the past.

If it is true that God could have held the usual laws of nature in abeyance, then all our efforts to understand our world would be frustrated. It would lead us to believe that nothing happened when, in fact, something remarkable did happen. The believer is committed to the proposition that in creating us God also endowed us with reason and the ability to draw conclusions. If God does things that frustrate our understanding, then it would then be difficult to escape the conclusion that God has deceived us. If God did this in Joshua's case, then how many other times has He stepped in to rearrange things? We cannot tell because, by the terms of the hypothesis, the results of His activities are undetectable. We might put it in vulgar fashion by saying that He always cleans up after Himself. If we accept the possibility that God can rearrange the laws of nature at any time, then we have to face the consequence that nothing can count as evidence for anything. In that case we must give up all intellectual activity; we simply can't say anything about the world at all. The English philosopher Bertrand Russell once posed this puzzling question. How do you know, he asked, that the world and everything in it, including your memories, did not come into existence five minutes ago? If we follow Archer we may as well say that, for all we know, God created the world 30 seconds ago including you and all your memories.

Archer does give us one additional bit of "evidence" in favor of the belief that the sun stood still. Astronomers at Harvard and Yale, he says, have discovered that a full day is missing from their astronomical calculations. He then adds that these reports have not been confirmed because those universities have preferred not to keep such records. Let us note three points about this contention. The assumption that astronomers have attempted to keep count of each day in the history of the earth, i.e. count each revolution of the earth, is preposterous. There is also the insinuation that our major universities are anti-Christian to the extent that they will suppress any evidence of a Biblical miracle. The third point is logically more interesting in its assumption that there is evidence to suppress.

There is a kind of position that is sometimes taken that can be called, in a pejorative sense, "conspiracy theory." Roughly, a "conspiracy theory" is a contention that something remarkable (and imaginary) is true, but the information about it is being withheld from us for one reason or another, usually sinister. When it is pointed out to such "conspiracy theorists" that there is no evidence that anything is being withheld they reply that this fact only shows how deep and sinister the "conspiracy" really is. It is like this with the curious belief that the United States Air Force has captured a UFO and is keeping it hidden somewhere in a mysterious hangar. The fact that there is no evidence whatsoever that this is the case is taken to prove how successful the government has been in keeping its secret. Likewise, in the not very distant past we were told that there was a communist conspiracy to overthrow the government of the United States. The lack of evidence for any such untoward activity only confirmed the depth of the unholy conspiracy in the eyes of the true believer. Archer's complaint about the conduct of the universities in the matter of Joshua's long day has all the marks of a "conspiracy theory."

This criticism of the doctrine of Biblical inerrancy is not introduced simply to dispose of an indefensible way of looking at things, but intended to draw our attention to some important lessons about the nature of inquiry and how we go about sifting the true from the false. We are the inheritors of an intellectual tradition that began with the Greeks and that has been developed and added to by innumerable generations of thinkers ever since. This tradition teaches us certain things about what it is to try to understand the world we live in and makes certain demands upon us. One of the most important demands that it puts upon us is that we practice intellectual responsibility. To be intellectually responsible is to be prepared to seek the truth and to get things right. It is to be prepared to withhold belief from any proposition for which there is either no evidence or insufficient evidence that it is true. It is to be prepared to offer appropriate reasons or evidence for any proposition that you claim to be true. The tradition demands that whenever we enter upon any investigation to find out whether some proposition or theory is either true or false we have some idea of what will count in favor of the proposition or what will count against it.

The hypothesis that God could have suspended the usual laws of nature in stopping the sun as well as imaginary conspiracy theories fail to meet this last demand. Ordinarily we would say that, if no evidence whatsoever is found in favor of a proposition, that proposition is no doubt false. Both of the views we have been considering, however, refuse to accept that conclusion. Archer refuses to allow anything to count against the truth of his contention. The emptiness of positions like these is brought home to us by Walt Kelly's comic-strip Pogo 'Possum. That observant creature once remarked that he had been raised by a tribe of invisible Indians and the fact that nobody had ever seen them was sheer proof.

Although many people have committed themselves to the belief that the Bible is true in all particulars even if they may not be aware that there is something known as the doctrine of Biblical inerrancy, very few have ever seriously considered the intellectual cost of that commitment. In order to maintain the belief in the complete truth of the Bible extraordinary logical gymnastics and sleights of hand must be pressed into service, and that requires us to give up the greater part of our intellectual standards.[10]

Modern Biblical Scholarship

The view of the Bible that has been achieved by modern scholarship is a sharp contrast to the conception of the Bible that we have talked about in the preceding section. The Biblical scholar asks the same questions about the

Bible that he or she would ask about any other document or piece of writing. When was it written? Who wrote it? Has it been modified or edited in its history? What was the historical situation in which the work was produced? What was the author's purpose and point of view? What audience was being addressed? The study of the Bible with the aim of answering such questions as these has been termed the "higher criticism." The higher criticism stands in contrast to what is called the "lower criticism" which is the study of the texts themselves, their variations and transmission.

The word "criticism" can seriously mislead a present-day reader who usually assumes that criticism is fault-finding. It is thus all too easy for many religious people with a respect for the Bible to shy away from such scholarship because they mistakenly believe that its intention is to discredit the Bible. With respect to serious scholarship, however, the word "criticism" means only a detailed and rational examination. What kind of ultimate judgment about the value of a work will eventually result from a process of criticism cannot be decided before the investigation. As a matter of fact, most Biblical scholars have been devoutly religious people, both Jews and Christians. Their aim has been not to discredit the Bible, but to understand it.

The Bible, including both Old and New Testaments,[11] is not properly speaking a single book, but is a collection of writings of very different kinds. The books that make up the Jewish Bible are divided into three parts. These are called Torah (Teaching), Nevi'im (The Prophets), and Kethuvim (The Writings). The entire collection is sometimes called Tanakh which is an acronym made from the names of the three divisions. The name *Bible* comes from the Greek word for book and was introduced early in the

Christian era. The earliest writings that make up the Jewish Bible date from some time probably not earlier than about 900 BC. The last book of these scriptures to be written was Daniel, which dates from the 160s BC during the time of the Maccabean revolt again the Greek tyrant Antiochus. The oldest material in scripture is found in parts of the five books of the Torah (or Pentateuch).

An important step in the creation of the book we know as the Bible was determining the canon, the official collection of writings to be included in the Bible.[12] By 400 BC the books that make up the Pentateuch had been accepted as canonical, that is, as sacred. By 200 BC the books of the prophets had achieved canonical status. There were, however, a number of other books in circulation that had a claim to be accepted and between about 200 BC and AD 200 a large number of writings of a religious nature were produced. It was not until the 90s of the first century AD that a final decision was made about which writings were to be admitted into the canon.

The canon of the Jewish Bible was accepted by Protestant Christianity although it changed somewhat the order and arrangement of the books. The Catholic Old Testament includes several books that are not in the Jewish canon. These books are known as the Apocrypha. The many other writings that never received canonical status are known as the Pseudepigrapha.

The Pentateuch posed special problems of understanding and Biblical scholarship had its beginnings in a question about the authorship of those books. A very old tradition claimed that Moses was the author of them. This tradition was seriously challenged in the seventeenth century when it became evident that there was much in the Pentateuch that could only have been written long after the time of Moses. During the eighteenth century investigators came to believe that the Pentateuch was actually a compilation of more than one document. This way of thinking about the composition of the Pentateuch was given its fully developed form in the late nineteenth century and is known as the documentary hypothesis.

This belief was based on a number of interesting facts about the text. There are two names used for God, Yahweh and Elohim. There are two versions of many stories. Scholars call these doublets. The name of the same person sometimes varies between the different versions. The location of the events also sometimes differs from one version to the other. There are definite stylistic differences in the way the language is used. When all these facts are looked at systematically it would appear that there must be two separate, although similar, traditions that have been combined into a single set of documents. Scholars call the tradition that uses the name Yahweh the J document and the one that uses the name Elohim the E document.[13]

These two documents were produced in the period of the division of the Israelite kingdom after the death of Solomon. J is a product of the southern kingdom of Judah and probably dates from 900 or after. E was composed in the northern kingdom of Israel about a century later. Both documents incorporate material from much older traditions. The two documents seem to have been combined into a single text around the middle of the seventh century. About the same time the greater part of the book of Deuteronomy was composed. Scholars call this the D document.

Some time after the Babylonian Captivity, perhaps 500 BC, a fourth document was written. This is the priestly code or P. Genesis 1 to 2:4 belongs to P as does the book of Leviticus. Eventually all four documents were combined to make up the Pentateuch as we know it. The documentary hypothesis is this thesis that the first five books are a composite of at least four different documents.

The Christian New Testament presents its own special problems to scholars. At the core of the New Testament is, of course, the figure of Jesus. It is impossible to date the life of Jesus with any precision. The best guess seems to be that he was born about 6 BC and was executed perhaps in AD 30. The earliest Christian writings that have come to us are the letters of Paul which date from the 50s, twenty years or more after Jesus' death. Paul did not know Jesus and tells us virtually nothing about his life. The gospels themselves do not provide us with a clear and consistent account of the life of Jesus. While there are two or three references in Roman literature of the late first century to the existence of Christians, there is no mention of Jesus from sources other than the Bible during the first century.[14]

Scholars are in general agreement that the earliest gospel is that of Mark and that the gospel of John was more than likely the last to be written. Mark was very probably not written before AD 70 and John was completed before AD 100. Although the names given to the authors of the gospels are those of people associated with Jesus and his ministry we have no idea who the actual authors were.

The three gospels of Mark, Matthew, and Luke are called the synoptic gospels because they are capable of being looked at, read together, and compared with one another. John is rather different from the synoptic gospels and evidently belongs to another tradition about Jesus. There is a very interesting problem about the sources of the material that the authors of the three synoptic gospels drew upon. Much of the material about the life and teaching of Jesus in the gospels of both Matthew and Luke was taken from Mark. In addition to what they took from

Mark, both Matthew and Luke share other material that is not in Mark. This has led scholars to suppose that they made use of another source about Jesus. This hypothetical source is referred to as Q.[15] Finally both Matthew and Luke have some material that is unique to each and not found in the others. This suggests that, in addition to Mark and the hypothetical Q, each had his own special source of traditions about Jesus.

The authors of the gospels cannot be understood to be either biographers or historians in the modern sense. They would not have understood what it was to interview surviving witnesses or collect their memoirs, to consult the birth records in Bethlehem or Nazareth or the archives of the Roman government about the trial and execution of Jesus. Their interests were very different from those of the modern researcher. The gospels tell many stories about Jesus, but there are variations in these stories and they can be arranged in different orders. The stories of the birth of Jesus are inconsistent and so are the reports of the resurrection. Modern scholarship is hard put to sift out a reliable account of the life and teachings of Jesus from the material supplied by the gospels.

In the first decade of the twentieth century Albert Schweitzer, whom many know as a great Christian missionary and doctor, but who was also a fine organist and Biblical scholar, wrote a book titled *The Quest of the Historical Jesus*. Schweitzer's title calls attention to a problem that historical research has not solved. There is a consensus among scholars that it will be very difficult if not impossible to get behind the gospel stories in order to reconstruct the life of the historical Jesus. It is sometimes said, especially by Protestants, that the church rests upon the foundation of the gospels. From a strictly historical standpoint this is not true. The gospels are a product of the early church in the years after the death of Jesus. The gospels were apparently written in response to problems faced by the developing groups of Christian believers in preserving memories of Jesus and in defining their own positions.

By the second century there were many Christian writings in circulation, but no single collection that could yet be called the New Testament. Some of the nascent churches would know perhaps one of the gospels, but not the others. It was not until later in the second century that the four gospels that we know were collected and combined into one book. There was considerable disagreement about some of the books that eventually were made canonical. Revelations was one of these. It was not until about 400 that the present New Testament canon could be said to be fixed.

Excursus into Method, Logic, and Truth

It is now time to return to the question with which we began this chapter: Is the Bible true? The doctrine of Biblical inerrancy claims that the Bible is an historical document that tells us of very important events that have happened in the past. If this claim is to be taken seriously, then whatever is said in the Bible must be tested and examined in the way that any other historical document is tested and examined. Over the centuries our western intellectual tradition, beginning with the Greeks, has developed methods of scientific and scholarly investigation designed to distinguish the true from the false, the possible from the impossible, and understanding from ignorance. We know how to determine whether statements are true or false and we know how to test theories and hypotheses for their adequacy and explanatory value. How does the Bible stand up to this kind of examination?

Before we can approach the question of the truth of the Bible we have to do two things. The first is to say something about the notion of truth. We use the word "truth" in a number of different ways. We can speak of a true friend or a true Englishman. In the first case "true" is synonymous with "loyal" and in the second case can suggest "characteristic" or "typical." The carpenter trues the frame of the house, that is, he makes it square. A true likeness is a portrait that resembles its subject. We also speak of what someone says as true. When we say that he spoke the truth, we usually mean that the statement he made, the proposition he uttered, is true. This is the sense of "true" with which we will be concerned.

Truth, as we are concerned with it, is a property of statements or propositions. It is only of propositions that we shall ask whether they are true or false. Our question can now be put in this way: Are the propositions asserted in the Bible true? Before we can answer this question there is one more thing we must do.

We have already seen that the Bible is a collection of many different books and now we must note that these books contain a number of different kinds of material. There are historical records of the kingdoms of Israel and Judah. There is a great deal of poetry in the Jewish Bible which English translations tend to obscure by rendering much of the poetry as prose. There are moral commandments and there are instructions for the performance of rituals. There are exhortations to Israel to be faithful to God. There are prayers and proverbs and there are stories that were surely meant to be taken as tales to be read for both enjoyment and edification.

The conclusion to be drawn from these facts is that not all of what is said in the Bible consists of propositions and so not all of what is in the scriptures is to be judged in terms of whether it is true or false. We do not usually think of poetry as either true or false. Laws, commandments, and exhortations are imperatives and not statements, and imperatives, of course, are neither true nor false. Stories and tales can be enjoyed without concern for their truth. The question of truth naturally arises when something is represented to us as reports of facts and as history.

In his widely circulated book, *The Bible as History*, Werner Keller describes the extent to which archeological and historical investigations have confirmed accounts in the Bible. After reflecting on these modern results he says, "I thought of the skeptical criticism which from the eighteenth century onward would fain have demolished the Bible altogether, there kept hammering in my brain this one sentence: 'The Bible is right after all!' "[16] This claim can be very seductive, but we have to compare what the proposition seems to assert and what the results of modern investigation have actually revealed.

Keller's claim seems to put him in the camp of the Biblical inerrantists, but the archeological results that he describes to us do not support that position. In the 1920s archeological digs at the site of the ancient city of Ur, the alleged home of Abraham, revealed a thick layer of mud and silt that could have only come from an ancient flood of considerable extent. Subsequent investigations showed that this flood extended over a good bit of Mesopotamia. It was tempting to identify this with Noah's flood.[17] A little reflection, however, shows that identification does not work. An extensive flood in ancient Mesopotamia is not the flood described in Genesis 7: 19–20 in which "all the highest mountains everywhere under the sky were covered. Fifteen cubits higher did the waters swell, as the mountains were covered.' What the archeologists had discovered was anything but a world-wide flood. Ironically, the best that these discoveries can do is to allow us to speculate that the archeologists' flood may have been the basis for the various flood legends of the ancient near east and that can give scant comfort to the doctrine of inerrancy.

A second example brings us closer to what is really the crucial problem. In 701 BC the Assyrian king, Sennacherib, invaded Judah and besieged Jerusalem. That much is known from Assyrian inscriptions. Apparently on the point of victory, the Assyrians abandoned the siege and marched away. The Biblical account explains this delivery by the fact that "an angel of the Lord went out and struck down one hundred and eighty-five thousand in the Assyrian camp, and the following morning they were all dead corpses" (II Kings, 19:35).[18]

History can establish the fact that the Assyrians besieged Jerusalem and then gave up the siege, but can historical investigation establish that it was the result of divine intervention? More generally, can any factual, that is empirical, inquiry ever determine that an event is caused by God or any other divine agency? It is conceivable that evidence could turn up to show that the Assyrian retreat resulted from a plague that decimated the army. Some have thought that this is the proper explanation. Could we, however, imagine evidence that the plague was visited upon them by God? If anyone thinks this can be done, he or she must describe very carefully and specifically what sort of evidence this would be. It is by no means clear what that evidence would be. The account in Kings is evidence that at least some people *believed* that God had delivered Jerusalem from the Assyrians, but what is at issue is not what anyone believed; it is, rather, the *truth* of that belief.

Historical scholarship and archeology can confirm much in the chronicles of the kingdoms of Israel and Judah concerning their various kings, their relations with foreign powers such as Assyria and Egypt, and the like. It can confirm that the way of life of the patriarchs described in Genesis is based on reasonably accurate portrayals of what life must really have been like in parts of Mesopotamia in the second millennium before the Christian era. It would take a very special argument, however, to show that historical scholarship can establish that God or any other divine agency was active in any of the events described. That is, it would take a very special argument to establish that the empirical methods of historical research can show any religious significance in the events described. No such special argument has as yet been provided.

The Bible is of the greatest religious significance. That cannot be doubted and historical scholarship need not doubt it although it cannot confirm it. We will have to ask about the source of that significance and that question becomes another in that little budget of loose ends to be tied up in a later chapter. For the time being let us note that there is apparently a logical gap between the historical statement that the Assyrians abandoned the siege of Jerusalem and the religious claim that it was God's doing. If we put it in the form of an argument that gap becomes obvious:

> The Assyrians abandoned the siege.
> ___
> Therefore God caused them to abandon it.

It should be clear that no further historical evidence can close that gap.

This can suggest to us that there is an important difference between religious statements and statements of historical and empirical fact. The doctrine of Biblical inerrancy obscures this difference when it claims that every statement in the Bible is true without distinguishing statements with religious significance from statements of ordinary fact. It puts them all on the same logical level and leads the inerrantist to make what appear to be factual claims although they are claims that cannot possibly be confirmed.

At this point it will be useful to compare the method of the scholars who developed the documentary hypothesis with the method of Biblical inerrantism. The Biblical inerrantist begins with the assumption that every statement in the Bible is true and then has to show that what appear to be inconsistencies in the text are not inconsistent at all. In order to do this, however, the inerrantist has frequently to ignore what the text actually says or engage in purely *ad hoc* interpretations or explanations.[19] Since it is committed ahead of time to its conclusions, Biblical inerrantism must refuse to allow any evidence to count against its views. Any facts about scripture that would tend to show the doctrine to be mistaken will be ignored, discounted, or explained away. It will have to dismiss the documentary hypothesis as a *mere* theory, a mere guess, that has no substantiation and flies in the face of what are taken to be the facts.

If you wish to disagree with the findings of modern Biblical scholarship you must challenge scholars on their own grounds. That is, you must make use of the same methods and the same kinds of evidence that they do. You will have to show that this particular passage was mistranslated, that this particular conclusion conflicts with what is known from other sources, that there is new evidence that has not been taken account of and a host of other details of that nature. Fundamentalists do not do this. They are not concerned to engage in detailed objective examination and evaluation of the evidence. Their initial stance forbids them to do this; they have committed themselves to the outcome of the investigation before it is started. No honest inquirer, whether in science or in historical scholarship, can decide the outcome of an investigation before it starts. You must go where the evidence leads whether you like it or not.

Here is a place where the failure to understand the nature of theory as we explained it in chapter 1 works mischief. A theory is not an unsubstantiated speculation or guess about what the facts are, but is an attempt to make sense of and explain the facts. That is what the documentary hypothesis does. The facts to be explained are such things as the different versions of what are essentially the same stories, the different names for God, the different place names that figure in the stories and the different literary styles found in the varying tales. Biblical inerrancy denies that there are any such differences to be explained.

The documentary hypothesis is not at all *ad hoc.* It has identified systematic variations that call for explanation in terms of the combining of different sources. It is subject to confirmation or rejection in terms of new evidence. Should hitherto undiscovered manuscripts or archeological discoveries come to light it is altogether possible that the hypothesis would receive further confirmation, or that it would be shown to be mistaken in some respect and have to be revised or possibly even given up altogether.

Biblical inerrancy is a *doctrine* to be held on faith that admits no modification. Modern scholarship, by contrast, seeks the most probable theory that will make sense of the evidence. Evangelical fundamentalism and the doctrine of

Biblical inerrancy that it spawned arose in the first half of the nineteenth century out of a philosophical background that has to be taken seriously. It was not, therefore, in its beginnings anti-intellectual. This philosophical tradition, from Francis Bacon through John Locke to the Scottish "Common Sense" thinkers, never properly understood the direction that modern science took and as a result never understood the nature and role of theory in scientific explanation. The movement became completely out of touch with modern science and the specialized knowledge and methods that both natural science and historical scholarship came to make use of. It both resented and distrusted this specialized knowledge that was out of reach of the average believer. Fundamentalism ended by becoming anti-intellectual and by making a cult of scientific and scholarly ignorance.

At last we are in a position to provide an answer of sorts to the question with which we began this chapter. To investigate the question of the truth of the Bible we had to sort out the propositions in the Bible from other kinds of material and then we had to make a distinction between propositions with religious significance and more ordinary ones. With respect to the more ordinary ones we can say that extra-Biblical evidence suggests some are true and some are not true and then there are some that we do not have the evidence to permit us to decide. But when people are concerned to know whether the Bible is true it is almost always because their concern is religious and not historical. There are probably very few people who really care about setting the historical record of Judah's relation with Assyria straight. When people ask "Is the Bible true?" there are invariably asking "Is the Bible the true record of God's relation with mankind and does it tell me what I must do in order to live properly or to achieve salvation or something of that sort?" We have the methods of historical and archeological investigation for evaluating the truth of the historical portions of scripture, but we have no comparable methods for answering the latter question, the one that is really on people's minds.

Suggestions for Further Reading

Fundamentalism

For the history of the fundamentalist movement in the United States see Ernest R. Sandeen, *The Roots of Fundamentalism* (Chicago: University of Chicago Press, 1970), and George M. Marsden, *Understanding Fundamentalism and Evangelicalism* (Grand Rapids, Mich.: William B. Eerdmans Pub. Co., 1991). The role of Scottish Common Sense Realism and Baconian philosophy of science in the history of fundamentalism is detailed by George M. Marsden, *Fundamentalism and American Culture* (New York: Oxford University Press, 1980).

Modern Biblical scholarship

There is a seemingly endless variety of books that explain the results of Biblical scholarship in more or less non-technical ways. Here is a sampling of some of them. Most of them have extended bibliographies that will point you to the specialized work of scholars.

One general guide is Robert Alter and Frank Kermode, eds, *The Literary Guide to the Bible* (Cambridge, Mass.: Harvard University Press, 1987). *The Interpreters Bible*, 12 vols (New York: Abingdon Press, 1951–7), provides a translation with detailed commentary. *The Oxford Study Bible* (Oxford: Oxford University Press, 1992) contains very helpful articles on the Bible and its background. it also includes the Apocrypha.

On the Jewish Bible (the Old Testament), see Bernard W. Anderson, *Understanding the Old Testament*, 3rd edn (Englewood Cliffs, NJ: Prentice-Hall, 1975). Harold Bloom, *The Book of J* (New York: Grove Weidenfeld, 1990), is a fascinating attempt to reconstruct the J document and speculate about its authorship. See also Richard Elliot Friedman, *Who Wrote the Bible?* (New York: Summit Books, 1987); John B. Gabel and Charles B. Wheeler, *The Bible as Literature*, 2nd edn (New York and Oxford: Oxford University Press, 1990); Otto Kaiser, *Introduction to the Old Testament* (Minneapolis: Augsburg Publishing House, 1975); Woodrow Ohlson, *Perspectives on Old Testament Literature* (New York: Harcourt Brace Jovanovich, 1978); and D. S. Russell, *The Old Testament Pseudepigrapha* (London: SCM Press, 1987), which is a good introduction to the nature and content of the Pseudepigrapha.

On the New Testament, see Hans Conzelmann, *History of Primitive Christianity*, trans. John E. Steely (Nashville: Abington, 1979); Gaalyahu Cornfeld, ed., *The Historical Jesus* (New York: Macmillan, 1982); A. Powell Davies, *The First Christian* (New York: Mentor Books, 1957), an examination of Paul and the problems of understanding early Christianity; Michael Grant, *Jesus: An Historian's Review of the Gospels* (New York: Charles Scribner's Sons, 1977); R. Joseph Hoffman, *Jesus Outside the Gospels* (New York: Prometheus Books, 1984); R. Joseph Hoffman, ed., *The Origins of Christianity* (New York: Prometheus Books, 1985); and Howard Clark Kee, *Jesus in History* (New York: Harcourt, Brace & World, 1970). John P. Meier, *A Marginal Jew* (New York: Doubleday, 1991), is an excellent and up-to-date examination of what can be known about the life of Jesus. Norman Perrin and Dennis C. Duling, *The New Testament*, 2nd edn (New York: Harcourt Brace Jovanovich, 1982), is a very useful account of New Testament scholarship. See also Elaine Pagels, *Adam, Eve, and the Serpent* (New York: Random House, 1988) and *The Gnostic Gospels* (New York: Random House, 1981); Jaroslav Pelikan, *Jesus Through the Centuries* (New York: Harper and Rowe, 1985);

Thomas Sheehan, *The First Coming: How the Kingdom of God Became Christianity* (New York: Random House, 1988); and Graham N. Stanton, *The Gospels and Jesus* (Oxford: Oxford University Press, 1989).

Notes

1 It is unfortunate for Ussher's reputation that he is known almost entirely for that calculation alone. He was an able and important scholar.

2 Reid's criticisms of the thought of Locke, Berkeley, and Hume are subtle and deep. What is important for our purposes, however, are not the details of his arguments, but the use that was made of his ideas by the nineteenth-century Princeton theologians whether or not they were correctly understood.

3 Quoted by George M. Marsden, *Fundamentalism and American Culture* (New York: Oxford University Press, 1980), p. 111.

4 Quoted in ibid., p. 113.

5 Gleason L. Archer, *Encyclopedia of Biblical Difficulties* (Grand Rapids, Mich.: Zondervan Publishing House, 1982).

6 Ibid., pp. 20ff.

7 There is sometimes debate about whether the Bible contains contradictions. Two propositions are said to be contradictory if they must have opposite truth values. "Man was created before the animals" and "Man was not created before the animals" are contradictory propositions; one of them must be true and the other must be false. There are probably few, if any, contradictory propositions in the Bible. Two propositions are said to be inconsistent if they cannot both be true. "Man was created first" and "Man was created last" cannot both be true, but both could be false. There are many such propositions in the Bible. Although

contradictory propositions are inconsistent with one another, they are not the only species of inconsistency.

8 Archer, *Encyclopedia of Biblical Difficulties*, pp. 68–70.

9 Ibid., pp. 161–2.

10 Archer's book is a wondrous budget of these intellectual tricks in its attempts to explain and explain away numerous curious phenomena and inconsistencies.

11 For the use of the terms "Old" and "New Testament", see chapter 1, note 12. The Jews, of course, do not accept the New Testament. For them the "Old" Testament just is the Bible. We will do much better to speak of it as the Jewish or Hebrew Bible. Since all but a small portion of it was written in Hebrew scholars sometimes use "Hebrew Bible" to refer to the book in the original language. When it is translated into modern languages it may be more accurate to speak of the Jewish Bible.

12 The word "canon" is derived from a Greek word which was itself derived from the Hebrew and means "rule." Applied to the Bible it refers to those books which "follow the rule" and are considered official.

13 In German "Yahweh" is spelled with a "J" and since so much Biblical scholarship is German in its origins it was only natural to use "J" to stand for that tradition.

14 There is one possible exception to this. The Jewish historian Josephus has a brief account of the arrest and trial of James whom he says was the brother of Jesus "who was called the Messiah" (Antiquities of the Jews, Book 20, ch. 9). Some scholars suspect the passage may be a Christian addition to the text. In Book 18 he devotes a whole paragraph to John the Baptist. Josephus wrote his book probably in AD 93.

15 The name "Q" is taken from the German word *Quelle* which means "source."

16 Werner Keller, *The Bible as History*, 2nd revised edn, trans. William Neil (New York: William Morrow & Co., 1981), p. 24.

17 Keller's colorful description of this is in ibid., ch. 3.

18 This is the subject of Byron's rollicking poem, "The Destruction of Sennacherib": "The Assyrian came down like a wolf on the fold, / And his cohorts were gleaming in purple and gold."

19 An *ad hoc* explanation is one designed for a single case alone and has no general application to any other case.

4

Religion and Science

Many people these days believe that there is some kind of conflict between religion and science. There are some religious people who reject one or another aspect of modern science because they believe that it conflicts with what is said in the Bible. There are scientifically minded people who reject religion because they believe that modern science has shown that many religious doctrines are false including what is said in the Bible. The focus of this dispute nowadays tends to be on theories of biological evolution. There are people who call themselves Creationists, and who are generally fundamentalists and Biblical inerrantists, that take their stand on the first chapter of Genesis which describes God as creating the world and all living things in six days. This stand leads them to reject any theory of biological evolution and any scientific theory that estimates the age of the earth in billions of years. This is an example of a conflict that goes quite beyond abstract intellectual disagreements because Creationists have tried to use the courts to force schools to teach Creationism as an alternative to standard science.

This controversy over evolutionary theory, however, is only the latest episode in a long history of relations between religion and science. Let us survey some of the high points in that history.

Religion and Science in the Ancient World

We mentioned in chapter 1 that there was already some conflict in the very beginnings of Greek science and philosophy between the new intellectual attitude and the older mythological accounts of the world that made up so much of the stuff of Greek religion. The philosopher Anaxagoras was tried in Athens about 450 BC on charges of impiety for teaching that the sun and moon were not gods, but natural bodies made of fire and earth. Socrates was also tried and executed on charges of impiety in 399 BC.

A very interesting example of one kind of relation between science and religion is found in the work of Epicurus who was active around 300. Epicurus accepted the theory of atomism that had been suggested as early as 500 BC. Atomism was the theory that everything is made of tiny material particles and all that happens in the world can be explained in terms of the behavior of these atoms. Epicurus, however, did not seem at all interested in detailed explanations of particular physical phenomena; his real concern was ethical. The principal cause of unhappiness, he said, is fear of the gods and especially fear of what will happen to us after death. Epicurus did not deny the existence of the gods, but he did claim that they had no concern for what goes on in the world. Natural phenomena should not be taken as expressions of either the gods' pleasure or their anger. They all have perfectly natural explanations. Death is the result of the dissolution of our atoms and leads to the complete absence of consciousness and feeling; thus death is nothing to be feared.[1] We have very little of the writings of Epicurus himself, but fortunately his views were borrowed and given lengthy expression by the Roman poet Lucretius (99–55 BC) in his poem *On the Nature of Things*.

Neither post-Exilic Judaism nor Christianity in its first centuries had any concern for science. Nor do we hear anything from the side of the Greek scientific tradition attacking either Judaism or Christianity for holding unscientific views. There were conflicts aplenty between early Christianity and the pagan world of Greek and Roman civilization in which it developed, but these conflicts were of a broad cultural, moral, and even political nature. They were not about science. It would not be fair to say that there was no science in late antiquity, but as a matter of fact the intellectual impetus that originated science in the Greek world had pretty well spent its force by about the third century of the Christian era. The philosophical interests characteristic of late antiquity tended to the moral and the metaphysical rather than the scientific.

During the last centuries of the western Roman Empire science was not a force to be reckoned with and in the centuries following the collapse of the western empire, the period we know as the Dark Ages, there was very little learning and intellectual life of any sort, let alone science. It may be worthwhile, however, to mention the fact that Justinian, the Christian emperor of the eastern half of the Roman Empire, closed the classical and pagan schools of Greek philosophy in Athens in AD 529. Many of the scholars became in effect refugees. Some found sanctuary in Syria, outside the borders of the empire, where they reestablished the teaching of the old science and philosophy. Whether or not this was a loss to Christendom, it was to prove a boon to Islam.

Religion and Science in the Middle Ages

In the seventh century Muhammad was able to unify the warring tribes of Arabia and to impose the new religion of Islam upon them. Like Judaism, to which it owes some debt, Islam is a monotheistic religion. Muhammad died in 632. After his death the Arabs began a conquest that spread Islam over a great deal of the ancient world. They moved north into the area of Palestine and Syria and challenged the power of the eastern Roman Empire.[2] They moved west across North Africa, into Sicily and into Spain. The attempt to extend their power north of the Pyrenees into France, however, was turned back at the battle of Tours in 732.

The conquest of Syria brought them into contact with the schools of Greek science and philosophy that Justinian had expelled from Athens. This was a very stimulating intellectual discovery for the Arabs and it was not long before a number of important centers of Islamic science and philosophy were established within their new territories. They made scientific advances in mathematics, astronomy, optics, geography, chemistry, and medicine that went far beyond the Greek foundations upon which they built. For most of the medieval period Islamic science was much more developed than anything known in western

Europe. Islamic philosophers, like their Christian counterparts, sought to use philosophy to provide intellectual support for religious beliefs. The major influence on this work was the philosophy of Aristotle. Names such as Avicenna (980–1037) and Averroes (1126–98) have a permanent place in every history of philosophy. There was a similar movement to reconcile philosophy and religion in medieval Judaism. Islam tended to be far more tolerant of the Jews than Christianity and many Jews rose to positions of prominence in both government and intellectual life. Schools of Jewish philosophy and scholarship nurtured influential figures such as Moses Maimonides (1135–1204).

The traditional religious mind of Islam had never been altogether comfortable with philosophy and science, and many believed that, instead of tailoring the science and philosophy of Aristotle to the beliefs of Islam, Averroes was modifying Islam to fit the philosophy of Aristotle. By 1200 there was a general reaction against philosophy. Here and there books were burnt and the study of philosophy was forbidden. Islamic philosophy and science went into a decline from which it has yet to recover. By that time, however, the intellectual baton had been passed to western Europe.

In the centuries immediately following the collapse of the Roman Empire in the west, intellectual life had almost ceased to exist. Little of the work of the Greek philosophers was available and Plato and Aristotle were not much more than names. By the beginning of the eleventh century, however, Europe was beginning to get back on its feet economically, politically, and intellectually. After this time there was an increasing amount of contact between the Christian west and the Islamic civilization of Spain. Jews frequently functioned as intermediaries in these contacts.

One most important result of these contacts was that during the twelfth century the works of Aristotle made their way from the schools of Islamic Spain to the scholars of the Christian west. These works had made a long and fascinating pilgrimage. They were, of course, originally written in Greek and then had been translated into Syriac after Justinian had closed the old schools. It was there that the Arabs encountered them and had them translated into Arabic. Translations were later made into Hebrew by the Jewish scholars. From Arabic or Hebrew versions they were translated into the Latin of the western thinkers. By the thirteenth century, however, much better translations had been made from the original Greek into Latin.

This western discovery of Aristotle was extraordinarily exciting. Aristotle had written on just about any subject that one might mention, logic, rhetoric, physics, metaphysics, astronomy, psychology, biology, ethics, politics, and who knows what else. A whole body of knowledge was suddenly revealed to the western scholars that they did not know existed. They were not long in making themselves masters of this material. The assumption was that Aristotle's work represented the truth about the created world and the task now was to reconcile what *reason* had revealed to Aristotle with what *faith* had revealed to Christianity. The great medieval synthesis of faith and reason was supplied by St Thomas Aquinas whose arguments for the existence of God we met in chapter 2.

This synthesis of Aristotelian science and Christian doctrine was given a marvelous literary expression in the great Italian poem *The Divine Comedy* by Dante Alighieri (1265–1321) of Florence. The poem, which was completed in 1318, is a record of man's spiritual journey through life as symbolized by a tour through the Christianized

Aristotelian universe. It is divided into three parts, *Inferno*, *Purgatorio*, and *Paradiso*. Dante describes how "Midway on the road of our life I found myself in a dark wood, whose direct way was blurred." He meets the Roman poet Virgil who tells him that the only way to find the true road is through hell and purgatory. He takes him through the gate that leads to hell over which is inscribed "All hope abandon, ye who enter here!"

Hell has the form of a pit beneath the earth that narrows as it descends, like an inverted cone with its apex at the center of the earth. The first circle of hell is limbo, a place reserved for all the great people of antiquity. Homer and the other great poets are there as are Socrates, Plato, Aristotle, and all the other famous philosophers. These men did not know Christ and so are not to be admitted into heaven, but neither are they to be punished. Dante would have liked to have stayed and talked with them, but he must go on with Virgil as his guide.

The further they descend into the pit of hell the worse are the torments that they witness. A number of the sinners they meet are figures from Dante's own day. Dante had been involved in some unfortunate political episodes in Florence that led to his exile with the threat of being burned to death should he seek to return to Florence. Some of the tortures that he depicts being visited on particular sinners are doubtless his way of taking poetic revenge upon his political enemies.

As they approach the bottom of the infernal region the fires of hell give way to cold and ice. At the very bottom of the pit, frozen into the ice and beating the air with his great wings, is Satan himself. He has three mouths and in each of his mouths he is eternally gnawing one of the three arch-sinners of history. Dante conceived treachery to be the greatest sin of all and the three worst sinners are thus the three arch-traitors of history, Judas, Brutus, and Cassius. Judas, of course, betrayed Christ and it was Brutus and Cassius who betrayed and murdered Caesar.

This linking of Caesar and Christ was a familiar medieval theme. Medieval Europe was dominated by Christianity and its institutions, but it was also haunted by the memory of the Roman Empire that had imposed order and peace upon the world before the chaos of the barbarian invasions and the Dark Ages and it maintained a vision of a reborn Roman Empire uniting the world under a single Christian emperor. That vision, however, was never to be realized. Although a political entity calling itself the Holy Roman Empire was established by Otto in the tenth century, it was later described by some wag as neither holy nor Roman nor an empire.

Dante and Virgil make their way past the body of Satan and once again reach the surface of the earth. They emerge at the base of the mountain of purgatory which is on the other side of the earth and diametrically opposite the city of Jerusalem. Purgatory is not much spoken of these days, but it is the place where sins may be atoned for, sins which are not as serious as the ones that condemn a person to hell. From hell, as we all know, there is no escape. At the top of the mountain is the earthly paradise, the Garden of Eden, that is now deserted. Here is where Virgil must say goodbye to Dante. Since he was pagan and not Christian he cannot take the next step that will lead to heaven.

From the top of the mountain of purgatory Dante ascends through the crystalline spheres that carry the planets around to the outermost sphere of the fixed stars and from there to the highest heaven beyond the stars which is the abode of God. There Dante experiences the beatific vision of God that cannot be put into words. Dante's journey is now completed. He has seen the entire universe and he has completed his spiritual journey from sin and suffering to atonement and finally to salvation.

Aristotle's scientific picture of the world lent itself very well to a Christian interpretation. The earth is the center of the world. Hell is directly beneath our feet and heaven is directly overhead beyond the outermost sphere of the fixed stars. This universe is not very big. There were no real estimates of the distance to the sphere of the stars, but it was not all that far away. We are poised here on earth between heaven and hell. Hell, to be sure, is rather closer to us than heaven, but heaven is altogether attainable. The earth is not only the center of the scientific universe, but also the spiritual center. It is the stage upon which the divine drama of salvation is being played out. In the beginning God created the heaven and the earth and placed man in an earthly paradise. Man disobeyed God, brought sin into the world, and was expelled from that paradise. But God so loved the world that in the fullness of time He sent His only begotten Son to redeem mankind and show the way to salvation. Some time in the future, probably not all that long off, the final curtain will be rung down upon this drama, the damned will burn in hell for ever and the saved will be transported to heaven and to a life of eternal bliss.

Religion and the Scientific Revolution

This tidy fit between Aristotelian philosophy and science and Christian theology could not long endure. It was already known in Dante's century that there were problems with Aristotle's physics and in a couple of centuries the ancient Greek astronomy would have to be revised. The Polish monk Nicolas Copernicus (1473–1543) worked out an astronomical theory in which the sun was taken to be the center of everything with the earth and the other planets revolving around it. Although Copernicus' theory attracted the interest of many scientists and pointed astronomy in the direction it was eventually to go, there were serious problems in it. These problems would require the work of seventeenth-century scientists such as Kepler, Galileo, and the incomparable Mr Newton before the theory could be put on a proper scientific basis. It then became clear that the earth was merely one of several planets orbiting the sun and the sun itself, far from being the center of the universe, was but one of a vast number of other stars in what may well prove to be an infinite universe.

The new scientific picture of the world that emerged in the seventeenth-century completely demolished the old medieval view and knocked the props from under the religious perspective that was accommodated to it. If the earth moves just like the other planets, then it cannot be the center of anything and there may be no reason for believing that humankind occupies the center of any stage or that we are playing out a drama of any sort. We can no longer say that heaven is above our heads beyond the sphere of the stars. If the universe is infinite, then there is no beyond and no place for heaven to be located. In that case hell is probably not in the middle of the earth either. If notions of heaven and hell were to be retained, they would have to be completely rethought.

It is no wonder that the new scientific developments of the sixteenth and seventeenth centuries met with a good bit of opposition from religious sources. It was not only the Roman Catholic Church that objected, but the new religious movements resulting from the Protestant

Reformation could often be hostile to the new science. We might mention the curious figure of Giordarno Bruno whom the Italian Inquisition burnt at the stake in 1600. His sins and heresies were too numerous to mention, but a contributing factor may have been that he had suggested at one time that the universe is infinite in extent. The most notorious case, of course, is that of Galileo whom the Inquisition squelched in 1633. In 1992 the Roman Church finally reversed itself and admitted that it was wrong to have condemned Galileo's views.

The civilization of the middle ages was dominated by religion whether it was Christianity, Judaism, or Islam. Regardless of which faith was accepted, this world was considered God's world and everything in it depended upon the will of God. From the scientific point of view this entailed that the ultimate explanation of all phenomena was the will of God. By the seventeenthth century, however, this way of looking at things began to change. It was during the seventeenth century that what we now understand as modern science took shape. The new science of the seventeenth century had two characteristics that set it apart from its ancestors.

It demanded that a scientific theory be empirically testable and that a theory be able to explain particular phenomena. It would no longer be enough to offer a general explanation of motion, but it would now be necessary to explain why, for example, the motion of a projectile follows the path of a parabola rather than some other path and why the orbit of a planet is an ellipse and not some other curve. The second characteristic was that the new science was to be mathematical. Its theories and laws must be stated in terms of mathematical relations between features of the world that could be measured and quantified and then calculated with. The scientific revolution of the seventeenth century culminated in Isaac Newton's *Philosophiae Naturalis Principia Mathematica* (*Mathematical Principles of Natural Philosophy*) of 1687.

It is obvious that no reference to God can enter into any of the mathematical formulae that are the expressions of the laws of physical science. This recognition did not, however, entail that scientists must give up religion. In fact, religious arguments were offered to explain why God was not to figure in science. René Descartes made important contributions to the seventeenth-century scientific revolution primarily by his invention of analytical geometry. In 1640 he published his *Meditations on First Philosophy* intended to provide both philosophical foundations and a program for the new mathematical physics. In *Meditation* IV he argued that, since God is infinite and incomprehensible to human reason and that since our natures are weak and feeble, we can know nothing of the purposes of God. It follows that "the species of cause called final [i.e. purposes], finds no useful employment in physical or natural things."

We can construct another argument to the same conclusion. Assume that everything that happens is the result of the will of God. The will of God is then a factor common to all phenomena and we can always, as it were, "divide through" by a common factor and cancel it out. If everything is the will of God, then it adds nothing to the description of a phenomenon to follow the description with the formula "and it is the will of God."

The success of Newton's physics gave rise to what has been called the mechanical view of the universe. We have already mentioned this in chapter 2 in connection with Cleanthes' argument for the existence of God, but now we must say something more about this mechanical view. If we know the position, the mass, the initial velocity of an object, and the forces acting on it at a given time, then Newton's laws permit us to calculate what its position and velocity will be at any future time. Newton's mechanics thus led to very precise descriptions and predictions of such things as the motion of projectiles and the motion of the planets. It was not difficult for the imagination of thinkers of this time to extrapolate from these successes to a much more daring speculation.

Suppose we knew the state of the universe at a particular time, that is, that we knew the position, mass, velocity, and forces acting on *every* physical particle in the universe. If we were to put all those numerical values into Newton's laws, then it would be possible, at least in principle, to calculate the complete state of the universe at any time in the past or any time in the future. In that case the universe would be a completely deterministic system. The state of the world at a given time would determine what its future states would be. No one, however, as a practical matter believed that this could actually be done. We could never acquire all the necessary information nor could we integrate the enormously complex equations that would be required for the calculations. Although we could not bring this off, it was assumed that God could for God is, after all, omnipotent and omniscient. It would capture the spirit of the age very well to say that for many intellectuals in the seventeeth and eighteenth centuries God played the role of the ultimate super-computer.

In this completely mechanical and deterministic universe there is very little, if any, logical room for God to act. Very few dared to doubt that God had created the world. He created the world as a great machine according to mathematical principles, endowed it with its initial charge of energy, and gave its particles their initial velocities. Once He had created the world and set it going there was no more for God to do but to sit back and admire His creation. The thing would run quite well without Him tinkering with it. This view that God created the world and set it going, but does not interfere in its affairs, is called deism.[3] Deism was a very popular view in the 18th century.

Let us take seriously for a moment this idea of the world as a great machine, that is, as Cleanthes put it,

> subdivided into an infinite number of lesser machines, which again admit of subdivisions, to a degree beyond what human senses and faculties can trace and explain . . . [and] are adjusted to each other with an accuracy, which ravishes into admiration all men, who have ever contemplated them.

We note an interesting consequence. If everything is so minutely adjusted to everything else, then a change in one part of the world must necessitate changes throughout the entire mechanism. When the engineer makes a slight adjustment in the valve setting of his steam locomotive the speed of the pistons is modified as are the forces on the crossheads, connecting rods, and eccentrics, the steam and coal consumption change, and so on. Likewise, if God is to act in the world, that is, if he is going to make alterations in any part of His mechanism, then corresponding adjustments will have to be made throughout the entire world mechanism.

This entails that if an individual prays to God to grant him a favor, that is, to change things for his benefit, he is, in effect, asking God to readjust the entire world machine for his personal benefit. And there is a real danger in this because certain requested modifications could easily destroy the very fabric of the world. To ask this of God was to the deist the worst possible expression of pride and impiety. The deist position on this is put very neatly by the English poet Alexander Pope in his *Essay on Man* in 1734.

> And, if each system in gradation roll
> Alike essential to the amazing Whole,
> The least confusion but in one, not all
> That system only, but the Whole must fall.
> Let Earth unbalanced from her orbit fly,
> Planets and Suns run lawless through the sky;
> Let ruling angels from their spheres be hurled,
> Being on being wrecked, and world on world;
> Heaven's whole foundations to their centre nod,
> And Nature tremble to the throne of God.
> All this dread Order break – for whom? for thee!
> Vile worm! – Oh madness! Pride! Impiety!
>
> (*I, 247–58*)

David Hume and the Argument Against Miracles

Another consequence of the deistic way of looking at God and the world is that it seems to rule out miracles, when miracles are thought of as extraordinary events that to all appearances run counter to the usual course of nature and in which God reveals his power. We think here of God speaking to Moses from the burning bush, a bush that was all aflame yet was not consumed, the parting of the Red Sea, the sun standing still for Joshua, Shadrach, Meshach, and Abednego coming unharmed from the fiery furnace heated to seven times its usual heat, Jesus turning water into wine[4] or raising Lazarus from the dead, and, what for

Christians is the greatest miracle of all, the Resurrection. There are religious people who would argue that the existence of miracles is a certain refutation of the deistic thesis that God does not act in the world, for how else are we to explain such events if not as the handiwork of God? We have already met this kind of argument in chapter 2.

Before we set out to explain what appears to be a Curious Unexplained Phenomenon, however, we must make sure that there really is a phenomenon to be explained. There were those in the eighteenth century who challenged the very existence of miracles. David Hume was one of these.[5]

In his *Enquiry Concerning Human Understanding* Hume devotes section X to the examination of the concept of a miracle. A miracle is first defined as a violation of the laws of nature and then modified to read "a transgression of a law of nature by a particular volition of the Deity." His discussion of whether there could be miraculous violations of the laws of nature presupposes the same empiricist principles that Hume puts in the mouth of his character Philo in *Dialogues Concerning Natural Religion*: all our ideas are derived from experience and all our reasoning concerning causes and effects is derived from experience.

Hume believes that our ideas of causal connections between events arise because in our experience certain events are always connected with certain other events. He gives us some samples of these connections: lead cannot, of itself, remained suspended in air, fire consumes wood, and water extinguishes fire. Laws of nature are then summaries of these uniform causal connections. There are other sorts of occurrences, however, whose connections are not that regular. Hume asks us to consider the connection between the reports that people give of events and the reality of the events themselves. By and large people do tell the truth about what they have seen, but we know that in many cases people make mistakes in their accounts of what happened and all too frequently people do tell lies.

Our only evidence, Hume says, for the occurrence of miracles is the testimony of other people and he asks us to consider the grounds upon which we accept the testimony of others. We accept without question the reports of, let us say, the assassination of Caesar, but we tend to be suspicious about the story of Joshua and the sun standing still. How is this difference in the reception of testimony to be explained? Hume asks us to look at the question as a matter of probabilities for, as he says, a wise man proportions his belief to the evidence.

In our experience we have discovered that people tell the truth about what happened a certain percentage of the time. That is, we have experienced there to be a positive correlation between the testimony and the reality of the event in some number of cases. This allows us to assign a rough probability to the truth of any report, but that probability will be less than 1 and will leave room for the possibility that the report is false. If the event reported is a very unusual or marvelous one, a kind that we have never heard of happening, the probability that it actually occurred is very low and we will be inclined to say that there is a greater probability that the report is false than that the event occurred. If the event is of a more ordinary sort, then the probability that reports of it are true is much higher. The report that astronomers saw a statue of Elvis on Mars is surely false,[6] but there is no such reason to reject the testimony about the murder of Caesar because the event is reported by otherwise reliable ancient sources and the assassination of dictators does occur with a certain frequency.

Suppose, however, that the event reported is not just rare or marvelous in nature, but is truly a violation of the laws of nature. The correlation that has been experienced in the past between the events described by a law of nature is 100 percent and the probability that an event will be followed by its usual effect is thus very close to 1. The probability of the law of nature being violated is then near to zero and any alleged report of it will have to be dismissed as more than probably false. Hume lays down as a general maxim for reports about miracles "That no testimony is sufficient to establish a miracle, unless the testimony be of such a kind, that its falsehood would be more miraculous, than the fact, which it endeavours to establish." Hume, in effect, is warning us to not to believe any story unless the probability that the storyteller is telling the truth outweighs the probability that the event never occurred. He makes it clear that he believes that there has never been the kind of testimony it takes to certify the story of a miracle. Although Hume's reasoning cannot rule out the possibility that there may be violations of the laws of nature and hence miracles, he can conclude that there has never been the slightest evidence that miracles have in fact occurred.

Hume's essay on miracles inoculates us with a healthy injection of skepticism against the many outrageous and fraudulent claims, both pious and secular, which we constantly encounter from many different sources. There are, nevertheless, a couple of serious difficulties with his thesis about miracles. In the first place, there is something odd about speaking of *the* laws of nature. As far as we are concerned, there are a great many things that scientists call laws of nature and these can be given up or modified and new ones get discovered from time to time. Even so, Hume's conception of natural laws is inadequate. Laws of nature, as they are understood these days, are not simply generalizations about regularities that we meet in experience.

Consider Boyle's law relating the pressure, volume, and temperature of gases ($PV/T = K$) or Newton's second law of motion relating force, mass, and acceleration ($F = ma$). It is simply not true that every time these quantities are measured the results agree with what the laws predict. It is quite likely that many of the "experiments" conducted in elementary science classes do not get results that agree with the laws. Fortunately, we do not take these results to show that the laws are not true. Rather we explain the discrepancies by citing poor experimental techniques, inadequate measuring instruments or the like. Even when the experiments are carried out with the greatest care there can still be results that do not agree with the laws. The practice of scientists is then to look for some force or other factor that is influencing the outcome rather than to abandon the law as false.

Sometimes, of course, phenomena are observed that simply cannot be accounted for in terms of the known laws of nature. Scientists do not consider such anomalous phenomena as either marvels or miracles. Instead, they conclude that the present laws and theories are inadequate and then seek to formulate theories and laws that will accommodate the new phenomena. The point of these remarks is to suggest that it is not at all clear what a violation of the laws of nature might be. For a phenomenon to be a genuine violation of the laws of nature it would have to be utterly resistant to scientific explanation for now and always and we have no idea how to recognize anything like that.

The events that are reported as miracles, however, are not like the anomalies that scientists frequently encounter in their work. Miracles are one-time events that do not stay around so that they can be studied. Scientific anomalies are repeatable in laboratory experiments or are there for continued observation like newly discovered astronomical phenomena. Scientific anomalies are of interest to scientists because they present challenges to current theorizing, but generally arouse no more than idle curiosity in other people. Miracles, by contrast, purportedly inspire awe and religious fervor in those who are said to witness them, not to mention those who hear tales of them. They are, after all, supposed to be the work of God and to reveal God's power or God's love.

An important aspect of miracles, or the reports of them, then, is the reaction people have to them. Let's take another look at miracles with this point about reactions in mind. Suppose that one of the Biblical miracles really did take place, the raising of Lazarus, say, as described in John 11. Also suppose that Lazarus was really dead and not just in a coma or some other state that could be mistaken for death. At the call of Jesus he comes from the tomb restored to life and we may suppose it is genuine life and not just the existence of a zombie or whatever fantasy a science fiction writer might create. John says that many who witnessed it believed in Jesus, but some went to the Pharisees and told them what Jesus had done. It was agreed by these latter that by doing such things Jesus could become a political danger. The story makes clear that for some the event was of great religious significance and that for others it was not. The gospel story does not describe anyone doubting that the event took place. Now imagine two of the witnesses to these proceedings. One of these scratches his head and says to himself, "Well, I'll be! Darndest thing I ever saw in my life. It sure beats that two-headed calf at the state fair!" He then goes home and tells his wife about it. (He wasn't one of those who went to the Pharisees.) The other observer falls on his knees and cries, "My Lord and my God!" He then picks up his cross and follows Jesus and his life is changed for ever.

Neither of our hypothetical observers bothered to ask whether or not the event was a violation of the laws of nature. Both did, however, take it as remarkable, but in quite different ways. For one it was simply a curiosity to be puzzled about and then filed away and eventually forgotten. For the other it was of the greatest religious significance, an event that changed his life and could never be forgotten. Only one of them would have described what he saw as a miracle.

Was it a miracle or only something very unusual? Note that as students of philosophy we do not have to take a stand on whether it really happened or not. Our business is to examine the *concept* of a miracle and is neither to accept nor to reject the story. Let us imagine being able to take Lazarus into the finest medical laboratory and run all manner of tests on him. If no explanation of his new animation is discovered, all that can be concluded is that at the present time there is no accounting for it. Suppose, however, a natural explanation of his return to life is found and presented to the believer. The believer may be disillusioned and throw down his cross in disgust at what he takes to be a trick that was played on him. If we think of miracles as violations of the laws of nature, then in the present case any rational person will have to agree that the raising of Lazarus was not a miracle and therefore had no religious significance. But must that be the believer's response? Might we nevertheless imagine him acknowledging the doctors' conclusions and then setting it aside as not relevant to his life? For him it remains a miracle.

This would give some people a reason for calling him irrational. They would argue like this: a miracle is a violation of the laws of nature and he agrees that, since there is a natural explanation, the laws of nature have not been violated. In insisting upon calling it a miracle he is contradicting himself and anyone who does that is irrational. The charge of irrationality obviously depends on that definition of a miracle. Recall, however, that Hume had added to his original definition of a miracle that it result from a particular volition of the Deity. A miracle is then an event in which the hand of God is present. Let's turn our attention to that aspect of miracles.

Whether or not an event is a violation of the laws of nature cannot be determined by any scientific investigation. Rather than classifying events as either in accordance with or in violation of the laws of nature it would be better to classify them as those for which there are at present scientific explanations and those for which at present there are not. The focus on violations of the laws of nature may have been a red herring. That is why it may be more enlightening to focus on the hand of God. But there remains a problem with that. There is no empirical test to determine that an event is caused by God and when we add that to the impossibility of determining when a violation of the laws of nature has occurred we see that there can be no natural or empirical criteria that allow us to identify anything as a miracle. There is no test that a disinterested observer, that is, an observer who has no stake in the outcome, can apply to decide that this event is a miracle while that other one is not.

Let us note that whether there has been a miracle is not a matter for a *disinterested* observer to decide. A miracle is an event with religious significance and we simply could not understand someone who agrees that this is a miracle and then remains disinterested. To believe that something is a miracle involves religious commitment. This is where a person's reaction becomes of the greatest importance. One person reacts to the event as a miracle and another does not. In this respect seeing an event as a miracle may be a bit like seeing that the sunset is beautiful. There are no criteria, no standards, no tests that we must apply to tell that it is beautiful. It just strikes us that way.

This emphasis on reaction has an interesting consequence. It cannot be decided ahead of time what kinds of events someone may find religiously significant. There is a tendency for many religious people, especially many Christians, to think of miracles in terms of spectacular events that defy the laws of nature, the sort of thing that was staged by Cecil B. DeMille, for example.[7] It is as if in order to be religious such people demand signs and wonders. There is, however, no reason *a priori* that the hand of God be revealed only in the spectacular. We should consider the possibility that the most commonplace events may be regarded as miracles, the birth of a baby, the blossoming anew of flowers in the spring, and perhaps the very world itself. The religious believer reacts to and understands the world differently than does the non-religious person. There is much more to be said about this kind of reaction and understanding, but that is one more item that waits further discussion.

If there is a conclusion to be drawn from this discussion of miracles it is that science cannot prove that miracles do not happen. Religion, on the other hand, cannot prove that they do and thus cannot say that there are things that science cannot explain. Here is a place where science and religion may pass one another by.

Evolution and Religion

Let's now leave the scene of eighteenth-century deism and return to the contemporary controversy in the United States that surrounds theories of biological evolution that we mentioned at the beginning of this chapter. The seed of the controversy was the publication in 1859 of Charles Darwin's *The Origin of Species*. Darwin was born in 1809, the son of one of the most distinguished medical doctors in Britain. Darwin studied medicine for a while, but was put off it in part by having to watch surgical operations as they were then conducted without anesthetics. He studied for the ministry and took his degree at Cambridge University. Although he had studied some biology as an undergraduate, he was by no means a professional scientist. Despite his lack of professional qualifications he was recommended to the position of naturalist on HMS *Beagle*, a ship of the Royal Navy, which was setting out on a five-year voyage of exploration and scientific investigation.

The voyage (1831–6) made a scientist out of Darwin. The vast range of both living species and fossil remains and the variations among them that he observed began to suggest new ideas to him. He returned to England with a vast collection of specimens for study and in the next decades began to develop his theory. He was reluctant to publish his work until he learned that someone else was about to publish a similar theory. Only then did he ready his own work for publication.

Darwin was aware from the evidence of fossils that species that used to exist no longer do and that species now living did not exist in the past. He had observed curious similarities between the anatomical structures of very different species and was struck by the variations to be found within individual species. His theory was designed to explain these facts. He concluded his "Introduction" to the *Origin of Species* by saying

> I am fully convinced that species are not immutable; but that those belonging to what are called the same genera are lineal descendants of some other and generally extinct species. . . . Furthermore, I am convinced that Natural Selection has been the most important, but not the exclusive, means of modification.

Darwin's theory explained the facts by the assumption that species evolve from other species and that natural selection is the principal mechanism that produces these changes.

The idea that species of living things do change over time was held by any number of people in Darwin's time. What made Darwin so important was that he developed the idea systematically, offered a mechanism to account for the changes, and provided the detailed evidence necessary to support the theory. Within a very short time Darwin's theory was accepted by the great majority of scientists as the only theory that made sense of the evidence.

Darwin's original theory has been much modified since his day. Contemporary evolutionary theory still retains natural selection as an important factor in species change, but supplements it with the results of Mendel's work in genetics and more recent developments in microbiology and biochemistry. Today it is incorrect to speak of *the* theory of evolution. No reputable biological scientist doubts that divergent species are the descendants of common ancestors, but there is a measure of disagreement about the mechanism that explains the changes. There is much more work to be done here and this is one thing that makes the frontiers of the biological sciences a very exciting place to be.

The religious objection to Darwin arose from views with a long history. The traditional Christian assumption was that the first chapter of Genesis was a true account of the origin of the world. That chapter tells how God created the plants and the animals and then created man to rule over them. The second chapter tells that Adam named the animals.[8] From this it was concluded that each kind of living thing was created individually by God, that they have not changed since God created them, and that man is special and very different from all the other living things. Since Darwinism claimed that species do change and that the origin of the human species is to be explained in the same way as the others, it was assumed that Darwinism was an attack on the very foundations of religion.

The conservative Christian reaction to Darwin was not necessarily hostile in the beginning. There were, and still are, plenty of theologians who argued that evolution could be understood as God's way of creating living things. By the 1920s, however, the battle lines were drawn and many fundamentalists came to believe that biological evolution was the great enemy of the Bible and the Christian faith.[9] In recent decades the opposition to evolutionary theory has been centered in something called "Creation science." Creation science takes its start from a literal reading of the first chapter of Genesis; it claims that the world is only a few thousand years old[10] and it argues that the conclusions of standard science are largely mistaken. It also claims that its position is genuinely scientific. Creation science would have been dismissed long ago as an intellectual aberration on a par with flying saucerism and Bermuda Triangle mysteries had it not been for its campaign to have Creation science given equal time with evolutionary biology in American public schools.[11] It thus became a political issue.

The Creationist strategy is not to provide any evidence for their views or any new way of making sense of the facts that evolutionary theory seeks to explain, but to argue that the conclusions of biology and geology are mistaken. Invariably these conclusions are either misunderstood or misrepresented. Unfortunately, these misrepresentations cannot be disposed of all at once because as soon as reputable scientists expose one confusion the Creationists invent another.[12] One example, however, will be enough for us to get a sense of the intellectual level of Creationism.

Two of the most basic principles of science are the two laws of thermodynamics. The first law is the law of the conservation of energy. It says that the quantity of energy in the universe is constant. The second law says that, although the amount of energy in the universe is constant, the energy available for doing work is continually decreasing. This is sometimes expressed by saying that disorder, or entropy, is continually increasing. Creationists claim that this second fundamental law is inconsistent with the existence of evolutionary processes.

The argument goes like this. Evolution postulates a development from the simplest single-cell organisms to the much more complex higher animals and man. This development requires ever increasing concentrations of energy. This concentration and increase in energy is presumably inconsistent with the second law of thermodynamics. Henry M. Morris, one of the prominent creationists, puts it like this.

> For the evolution of a more advanced organism, however, energy must somehow be gained, order must be increased, and information added. The Second Law says that this will not happen in any natural process unless external factors enter to make it happen.[13]

The obvious objection to this is that the second law of thermodynamics applies only to what is called a closed system, that is a system in which the amount of energy is constant. The universe as a whole is a closed system, but our earth is not. The sun pumps vast quantities of energy into it every day and living organisms are by no means closed systems; they take in energy in the form of nourishment. This objection makes clear that evolution is not inconsistent with the second law and thus disposes of the argument.

Morris acknowledges this objection, but does not have the intellectual honesty to admit his argument is mistaken. Instead of admitting the mistake, he switches to another argument. The argument, as it develops in the pages following the passage just quoted, is that the sun is capable of supplying *enough* energy for life, but that an additional factor must operate to *organize* the energy into the proper structure. Biological theory is presumably incapable of identifying that additional factor and, moreover, can never explain how living matter arose out of non-living matter. It should be obvious what Morris thinks this additional principle is. He says "The creation model emphasizes the unique origin of life, at the creative word of a *living* Creator. The scientific law of cause and effect requires the First Cause of life to be living!"[14] This is no more, and no less, than a variation on the argument from design. Hume demolished that in the eighteenth century.

It is tempting to speculate that, if science were better taught in American schools, Creationism would have no appeal. School textbooks too often present science as if it were a catechism, that is, a set of official questions to which there is a set of official answers. Science appears then as simply a set of propositions to be believed and we can well imagine someone preferring to believe the propositions offered by the Creationists. Creationism comes out of the same intellectual background as Biblical inerrancy; it puts the same emphasis on "common sense" and is equally suspicious of theory which it misunderstands as unjustified speculation. The proper teaching of science must make clear the nature of theory and how theory must sometimes introduce new concepts that seem to do violence to the "common sense" notions of everyday life.

No scientific investigation can decide what its conclusions will be prior to the investigation. It is an essential feature of science that its propositions and theories be testable and then accepted or rejected in terms of the test of evidence. If you wish to challenge a scientific theory or the conclusions of any scientific investigation, then you must use the techniques of investigation and the standards of evidence that characterize the scientific enterprise. It is as true of science as we saw it to be of Biblical scholarship that challenges must be issued and played out in the same intellectual arena. Creationism fails on all accounts. Its "conclusion" is a religious doctrine held on faith and any challenge to its views must be rejected *a priori*. The Biblical doctrine of Creation is not empirically testable and Creationists refuse to acknowledge scientific standards of evidence. Creationism is fraudulent science.

Science and Religion as Competitors

There can be a conflict between religion and science only if it is believed that the two are competing for the same prize. That prize, of course, is assumed to be the correct description and explanation of the phenomena of the physical world. The nineteenth century provided an interesting perspective on what it took this competition to be. The nineteenth century placed a great deal of stock in evolutionary thinking in general and not just in biological science. The influential German philosopher G. W. F. Hegel (1770–1830) formulated a grand theory of the whole of human history which he saw as advancing in stages motivated by Spirit striving to become conscious of itself. Karl Marx borrowed much from Hegel's ideas about the development of history, but stood it on its head and made the driving forces in human history material ones, primarily economic forces, rather than spiritual ones. The ultimate result of this historical evolution was to be a world-wide communist society.

More relevant for our purposes, however, was the work of the French intellectual Auguste Comte (1798–1857). Comte held an evolutionary view of the progress of human knowledge and understanding of the world. The intellectual childhood of mankind was the theological stage in which the world was thought to be governed by supernatural beings, gods. In the next, metaphysical stage, abstract metaphysical powers were substituted for the gods as explanations. This stage could be thought of as the intellectual adolescence of man. The metaphysical stage was eventually to be superseded by the age of what he called positive science. Science must reject ultimate explanations of either the theological or the metaphysical type in favor of the discovery of empirical relations between phenomena, a very Baconian or Humean conception of science. With the development of positive science mankind has reached its intellectual maturity. Neither religion nor philosophical metaphysics can explain the workings of the world and are ways of thought that must be outgrown before we can understand the world and ourselves properly.[15]

Even more important, and much more interesting, is Sir James G. Frazer's monumental *The Golden Bough*.[16] In this work Frazer traces connections between magic, religion, and science. He based his conclusions on numberless examples of practices reported in antiquity, on accounts of the practices and beliefs of primitives peoples of his time, and even on various ceremonies and rituals found in the Europe and Britain of his own day.

Frazer understands magic as an attempt to control the course of nature. The magician seeks to control such things as the sun and the rain, the growth of the crops, success in hunting or in battle and against one's personal enemies. Magic assumes that the phenomena of the world stand in definite causal relations to one another and that, if one can discover these connections, then one can achieve power over them. One of the principles upon which this assumption rests is that of homeopathic magic. Homeopathic magic assumes the principle that like causes like. At the time of the midwinter solstice, for example, when the hours of daylight are at a minimum it was in many societies the practice to burn fires in order to cause the sun to begin to shine longer. In order to harm an enemy it was believed that if one did harm to an effigy of the person comparable harm would befall the person himself.

As ages went by it began to dawn on some people that magic did not work. The sun would continue to increase regardless of whether the fire rituals were performed, and whether the rain fell or not seemed quite independent of the rain ceremonies. It was slowly realized that nature could not be coerced in the way that magic had assumed. This led to quite a new conception of why things happened as they did. Nature was not as uniform as had been thought and at times seemed downright capricious. The behavior of nature was not unlike that of a human being whose actions could be willful and anything but consistent. Thus was born the idea that the world does not run in a blind mechanical fashion, but is under the control of supernatural beings endowed with a will, in other words, gods. The age of magic gives way to the age of religion.

Frazer defines religion in terms of two characteristics: a belief in superhuman beings and an attempt to win their favor. The gods, or God, cannot be coerced as magicians believed they could coerce natural forces, but must be persuaded or induced to do what we want them to. Magic, however, did not altogether die out with the coming of religion; many magical practices lingered and sometimes became incorporated into religion itself. French peasants, for example, were said to believe that the priest had secret powers to control the weather.

One of Frazer's most startling claims is that magic and science share common assumptions about the nature of the world. They both assume that there are regular and lawlike connections between natural phenomena and that when these are understood nature can be controlled. The great failure of magic was that it completely misunderstood the nature of these connections. Only the empirical methods of science allow us to understand these correctly and to achieve a real measure of control over natural processes. Just as religion replaced magic so will science replace religion.

Frazer assumed that magic, religion, and science were all in competition, with the prize going to the one which could most accurately describe the way the world works and most effectively control the forces of nature. It is all too apparent that science wins that contest. It is, after all, science and the technology it spawns that dams the rivers to prevent floods, increases agricultural production, and mines the earth for sources of power. Frazer looked on the world from the perspective of a late nineteenth-century Englishman and that perspective was essentially utilitarian. That is, it was a perspective that regarded all rational human activity as aiming at some practical result. It was, to be sure, the perspective that created the industrial revolution and the British Empire.[17] And, we might add, it was an attitude toward things that was by no means confined to Great Britain. Since he thought of magic and religion as in competition with science, Frazer had to understand magic and religion as intended to achieve certain practical results by means of rituals, incantations, prayers, or combinations of these. Since these things never work to achieve the desired results, their practitioners must appear stupid, foolish, and naive.

The Golden Bough has had an enormous influence, not only on thinking about the nature of religion and its origins, but upon literature as well.[18] T. S. Eliot's *The Wasteland*, for example, a poem of twentieth-century spiritual emptiness, crisis, and renewal, borrows from Frazer's ideas. Frazer's work, however, has been the subject of much criticism. It has been claimed, and no doubt correctly, that the evidence he used to construct his theory was either unreliable or misinterpreted. Frazer was not a modern-day cultural anthropologist working in the field and living with the primitive peoples whose customs and ways he was describing and theorizing about. He was, rather, an "armchair" scholar who collected the tales of writers from antiquity and the reports of missionaries and other travelers who had written accounts of what they had seen in remote corners of the world. The ancient accounts were too often unreliable and certainly beyond the possibility of further confirmation. Many of the contemporary reports came from people who were not trained observers and whose European biases many times led them to misdescribe and misunderstand what they had seen. From the point of view of both contemporary anthropology and classical scholarship Frazer's methods and results will not stand scrutiny.[19]

There is, however, a much deeper, and philosophically more interesting, criticism of Frazer that was offered by Ludwig Wittgenstein.[20] The complaint that he got his facts wrong does not get at the real difficulty. Wittgenstein challenges the assumption that magic and religion are essentially utilitarian. In a very telling remark he says that "The same savage who, apparently in order to kill his enemy, sticks his knife through a picture of him, really does build his hut of wood and cuts his arrow with skill and not in effigy."[21] This comment reminds us that "savages" are not necessarily ignorant of the way the world works and that they are perfectly well aware of causes and effects in the course of their everyday life. They do not expect that sticking the knife through the picture is going to bring about the death of the enemy; they know what has to be done to kill a man. The ritual, therefore, most likely must play some other role than supposed cause. What that other role might be will have to wait for the last chapter.

In like manner, prayers offered by the religious believer are not always offered in order to achieve some practical result. When you pray "Thy will be done" you are certainly not asking God to grant any favors or to bring about some result that you desire, for the point of the prayer is to prepare you to accept whatever happens. Although the prayer "Forgive us our sins" may seem to be a request to bring about results, these results are in no sense utilitarian.

Frazer's evolutionary picture of the development of human understanding from magic through religion to science is surely mistaken. There is every reason to believe that he misunderstood some very important things about magic and he certainly did misunderstand much of what religion is all about. Like as not he misunderstood science, too. He represents science as if it is concerned solely with utilitarian results and that has the effect of collapsing science into technology. In the modern world there are very close connections between science and technology, but, as we saw in chapter 1, they are at bottom different things.

Some scientists and many scientifically minded people have said that religion is mistaken and that the religious believer is irrational, naive, or credulous for believing things when there is none of the evidence that either science or everyday common sense would demand for supposing them true. In the middle ages religion provided the dominant intellectual view of the world and philosophy (i.e. science) was thought of merely as the handmaiden of theology. The brief historical sketch that we have given of the relation between religion and science can leave the impression that ever since the middle ages science has little by little been crowding religion out of the intellectual scene so that these days there is very not much room left for it.

It is at this point that there is a temptation for the religious person to charge that science has its limitations and that it cannot explain everything. By this it is hoped that a little room can be found for religion in those areas where science fails. One of those areas concerns the existence of the world itself. Science can explain many things, it may be said, but it cannot explain the creation of the world. This is an obvious invitation to invoke God as the creator.

Where did the world come from? What is its origin? Was it created or has it always just been there? These questions are puzzling. Puzzling questions are not the same as difficult questions. There are some questions that we cannot now answer, e.g. Are there planets orbiting other stars? Is there a sequence of three 7s in the decimal expansion of pi? These questions will be difficult to answer, but there is nothing essentially puzzling about them. They are not puzzling because we know what an answer to them would be like and we may even have some ideas about how to find the answers. What makes the other questions puzzling and not just difficult? To see that let's look at some other questions about origins.

What is the origin of the lamp upon the table? That's an easy question. It came from the lamp factory where various pieces of metal and glass were shaped and assembled. We understand how to deal with questions of the form "What is the origin of ____?" Such questions are answered by recounting how appropriate raw materials took certain forms and came together. We can ask the question about the origin of the earth and the astrophysicists can tell us how various bits of matter came to have this spherical form although the astrophysicists may disagree in the explanations they give us. Note that it is not a question of whether any one of these astrophysical explanations is the true one. The issue concerns the intelligibility of the question and suggested answers to it. The question is perfectly intelligible and so are the answers regardless of which one is true. Only if a statement is intelligible can it be said to be false (or true). We can go on to ask the question about the origin of our solar system, our galaxy, and any other things in the world.

When we move to the question about the origin of the whole universe, however, something strange happens. The other questions demand answers in terms of pre-existing raw materials and all such raw materials are simply stuff that exists *in* the world and that is part *of* the world. But nothing like that is available to us when we ask about the origin of the world itself. There cannot be any raw material that exists independently of the world to form the stuff of the answer. Anything that exists must already be part of everything, that is, the world.

It is here that the believer may be tempted to say that just as the lamp makers made the lamp so God created the world (possibly with the qualification that He did it without having to use any raw material). If God is to be understood on the analogy of a workman, then the question naturally arises about who made God: Where did God come from? In that way of looking at it we are no closer to an answer. We have already met the old philosophical tradition that God is a being that necessarily exists; He is uncaused or, as they used to say, He is the cause of Himself. If we appeal to the existence of God to explain the origin of the world and then reject any explanation for the origin of God, we may as well say that the world is uncaused and stop there. That would save one additional theoretical step.

The question about the origin of the world has suddenly become very queer; we don't know how to answer it. You must not misunderstand that last remark. It does not mean that we don't know what the answer is. It is rather that we do not have any idea what kind of an answer we are looking for and consequently we could not recognize anything as an answer to the question. If we do not understand what could possibly count as an answer to a question, then we do not understand that question. This last remark is itself subject to misunderstanding. It is not that *we* do not understand the question as if there may be SOMEONE who does. There are surely branches of mathematics that readers of this book do not understand, but there are mathematicians that do understand them and if we worked hard enough, well . . . It just may be that no one can understand the question because the question may not be a genuine question at all. What we should realize is that the question has no application to the world as a whole.

With this question about whether science can explain the origin of the world we have encountered one kind of typical and traditional philosophical question. That kind of question is not just a difficult one, but is a puzzling one. Every answer proposed to it is unsatisfactory and we don't know where to turn next. This is where we must make use of some of the philosophical strategies we have used in the previous chapters. What we must do as philosophers is to look more carefully at the nature of the question itself and then we see that it is not just that the answer to the question is difficult to find or somehow beyond our abilities, but that the question itself is in some way illegitimate. We will have found that we were really engaged in a game of intellectual thumb catching.[22] We must come to see that there was something wrong in the task that we set ourselves.

Philosophy does not give us truths about the world; it is not a kind of science or natural history. Philosophy is not a kind of religion either or a substitute for religion. The aim of philosophy as it is expressed in these pages is to help us get our ideas in order and to get a better understanding of the questions we want to ask. We have already said that philosophy has something to do with concepts. In this chapter we have investigated the *concept* of science and under that heading we have considered such things as the nature of theory and explanation and how some religious people as well as scientists have misunderstood how these notions work. We have also said something about the *concept* of religion, but much remains to be said in the last chapter. We have, however, said enough to suggest that science and religion are different things and thus are not competing for the same prize. If that is so, then they cannot really be in conflict with one another.

Suggestions for Further Reading

Sensitive readings of both Lucretius and Dante are given by George Santayana in *Three Philosophical Poets* (Cambridge, Mass.: Harvard University Press, 1947).

A useful account of medieval Islam and its science and philosophy is in Will Durant, *The Age of Faith* (New York: Simon & Schuster, 1950).

There are several good books that explain evolutionary theory and detail the confusions of Creationism. The following are recommended. Philip Appleman, ed., *Darwin* (New York: W. W. Norton & Co., 1979); the article by Preston Cloud is especially good. Douglas J. Futuyama, *Science on Trial* (New York: Pantheon Books, 1983). Philip Kitcher, *Abusing Science* (Cambridge: MIT Press, 1982). Michael Ruse, *But is it Science?* (Buffalo: Prometheus Books, 1988) and *Darwinism Defended* (London: Addison-Wesley, 1982).

Mary Midgley, *Evolution as a Religion* (London and New York: Methuen, 1985), is an interesting study in the misunder-

19 These criticisms are detailed by Theodore H. Gaster in his "Editor's Foreword" and "Additional Notes" in his edition of *The Golden Bough*.

20 Ludwig Wittgenstein (1889–1951) was a Viennese-born philosopher who did much of his philosophical work in England. His major works include *Tractatus Logico-Philosophicus*, trans. D. F. Pears and B. F. McGuinness (New York: Humanities Press, 1963), originally published in 1922, and *Philosophical Investigations*, trans. G. E. M. Anscombe (New York: Macmillan, 1953).

21 Ludwig Wittgenstein, *Remarks on Frazer's Golden Bough*, ed. Rush Rhees, trans. A. C. Miles (Atlantic Highlands, NJ: Humanities Press, 1979), p. 4. The remarks in the book were written at various times between 1931 and 1948.

22 How to play thumb catching: Make a circle with the thumb and first finger of your left hand. Insert the thumb of the right hand through the circle. With the entire right hand reach around the circle and grasp your right thumb in your right fist before it gets away. If you are left-handed you may reverse the hands.

5

Religion and Ethics

Perhaps the most important questions that thoughtful people face are about how we ought to live our lives: What goals are worthy of being pursued? How should we behave with respect to other people? How should we evaluate the character of other people and our own character as well? These are questions that belong to that branch of philosophy called ethics, or moral philosophy.[1] Ethics investigates our standards of value and proper conduct and the distinctions we make when we describe a person, thing, or situation as good or bad and the actions we do as right or wrong. Everyone knows that there is a very close relation between religion and ethics. The major religions of the world all offer codes of proper conduct to their followers and encourage them to live in the ways taught by the founders and prophets of the religion. In this chapter we will explore two philosophical questions about the connections between religion and morality.

We can investigate the moral teachings of the various religions from several points of view. Their ethical codes can be described and compared and their histories and how they have changed over time can be traced. We can also investigate how various religious communities, churches, congregations, and the like, interpret those teachings and put them into practice; how they encourage their members to follow the teachings, how the children are taught, and how wrongdoers are admonished or punished. All of that, however, is the subject of history and the social sciences and does not yet get us to the specifically philosophical issues that it is our business to examine.

We have proceeded on the assumption that philosophy is concerned with conceptual questions and that is certainly true of much of moral philosophy. One task that moral philosophy has set itself is to investigate such basic ethical notions as "good," "bad," "right," and "wrong" and then to construct theories about what these words mean and whether the judgments of value that we make with them can be shown to be either true or false. One such theory is called theological ethics.

Another task for philosophy, and theology as well, is to explain the existence of evil in the world. Why, it has been asked, would a good God permit evil to exist in the world that He created? This is called the problem of evil.

Theological Ethics

Theological ethics seeks to discover some kind of *logical* relation between God and basic moral concepts. This is quite a different task than merely describing the moral views associated with religions or tracing their histories. Theological ethics attempts to *define* one or more moral concepts in terms of the commandments of God. Suppose we want to define the notion of a morally right action in terms of the will of God. Then to say that some action, say x, is morally right is to say that x is commanded by God. We can represent it like this:

x is morally right = df x is commanded by God

This definition would, at least in principle, allow us to determine the moral character of any action or verify the truth of any moral judgment that we make upon an action. It is merely a matter of determining whether or not an action of that kind is commanded or forbidden by God.

There are problems with this kind of ethical theory. In order to make use of this theory we must be able to determine in any case what it is that God commands, but how are we to determine what it is that God commands? One answer is that the will of God is made known in the scriptures, in the commandments and laws of the Pentateuch (generally referred to as the Mosaic law), or in the teachings of Jesus. The law, however, is neither complete nor consistent. It is not complete in that it does not address every possible circumstance in which a person has to determine the right thing to do. It does not, for example, say anything about the moral propriety of insider trading on the stock market, nor does it tell us what to do when balancing our concern to preserve the environment against the necessity of economic development.

One of the commandments says, "You shall not murder" (Genesis 20:13 and Deuteronomy 5:17).[2] The King James translation reads, "Thou shall not kill." There is an important distinction between killing and murder. Murder may be defined as wrongful or illegal killing and surely not all killing is either wrong or illegal. Killing an enemy in war or killing in self-defense is not generally considered wrongful. Deuteronomy 20:12–16, however, quotes God as saying when you capture a town by siege you are to kill all the men, but you can take the women and children as slaves. If the town is a neighboring one, the case is different, for then "you should not let a soul remain alive." The reason given, one that must seem rather lame to us, is that then there will no possibility that you will be corrupted by foreign influences from the conquered. This has to strike us as going a bit beyond the bounds of what ought to be permissible in warfare.

Everyone has to agree that murder is wrong; that, after all, is part of the meaning of the word. "Murder is wrong" is thus a tautology. While there can be no dispute about the wrongness of murder, there can be dispute about what cases of killing are wrongful and hence are cases of murder. People can be divided about that. A pacifist, for one, who believes that war is always wrong can easily think of killing an enemy soldier in battle as murder. Another may believe that killing an enemy is regrettable, but often necessary, and so is not murder. Reflection on the law has to leave us with an uncomfortable sense that the commandments are inconsistent in forbidding us to murder on the one hand and then enjoining us to slaughter innocent people on the other.

There are still further difficulties. Some of God's commandments do indeed have an unquestionably ethical content such as the prohibitions against murder, stealing, and adultery while others seem at best arbitrary or fanciful. We are told, "You shall not boil a kid in its mother's milk" (Deuteronomy 14:21), but this doesn't seem to have anything to do with what we ordinarily understand as morality. Nevertheless, according to the theory of theological ethics it has to be thought morally wrong because it is against the will of God. This should make us even more suspicious of the theory.

Christians may tend to believe that the will of God is made known through the teachings of Jesus rather than by the Mosaic law. The Christian doctrine of the Trinity identifies Jesus with God and from that it follows logically that whatever Jesus says is necessarily the voice of God. There is, however, a certain inconsistency in the teachings of Jesus, especially with respect to the Mosaic law. Jesus accepted the law, saying that "so long as heaven and earth endure, not a letter, not a dot will disappear from the law" (Matthew 5:18). There are, nevertheless, other passages where Jesus wants to modify or even reject portions of the law. The law of Moses identifies certain foods as "unclean" and not to be eaten, but Mark 7:19 reports of Jesus that "He declared all foods clean."[3]

To these scriptural difficulties we must add the fact that innumerable tyrants and murderers have sincerely claimed that God has spoken to them directly and that they were doing the will of God. We have to admit that there seems to be no obvious way to determine what is and what is not the will of God. Every claim that God commands this or that can be met with a counter-claim that He does not. There are no criteria available to us to settle such disputes.

These problems that we have identified about knowing the will of God are essentially *practical* obstacles to using theological ethics as a guide for making moral choices and evaluations. We must now explore a more philosophically interesting *theoretical* objection to defining morality in terms of the will of God.

This objection can be traced back to Plato's dialogue, *Euthyphro*. The subject of the dialogue is piety, but piety is understood to be a species of justice, a covering term for morality in general. Whatever is said about piety thus applies equally to notions of moral right and wrong. In his discussion with Socrates Euthyphro defines piety as what the gods love. Socrates then asks Euthyphro whether something is pious because the gods love it or whether the gods love it because it is pious. Euthyphro opts for the latter and thereby undercuts his own definition. We must understand how that happens. If you define piety as what the gods love, then you are saying that the word "piety" and the expression "what the gods love" have the same meaning. If they have the same meaning, then the claim that the gods love something because it is pious reduces to the truism that the gods love it because they love it. We are left to suppose that the notion of piety and the notion of what the gods love are two altogether different things.

In the eighteenth century the English philosopher Richard Price offered an argument that is logically similar to the objection Socrates brought against Euthyphro. He pointed out that, if morality is thought to be founded on the divine will (Euthyphro's "what God loves"), then "moral good and evil are only other words for . . . *willed* and *forbidden.*" If that were so, then "it would be palpably absurd in any case to ask, whether it is *right* to obey a command, or *wrong* to disobey it; and the proposition(s), *obeying a command is right*, . . . would be most trifling, as expressing no more than obeying a command, is obeying a command."[4]

Early in the twentith century a generalized formulation of this kind of argument was developed by the influential British moral philosopher G. E. Moore. Moore took the notion of "good" to be the most important moral concept, but he objected to any attempt to define it or otherwise analyze it. His argument depends upon the assumption that "whatever definition is offered, it may always be asked, with signifi,cance, of the complex so defined, whether it is itself good."[5] That is, it is always an *open question* whether the thing denoted by the definition is good. Let's see how this argument works with respect to a particular example.

There has long been an ethical theory called hedonism that defines good in terms of pleasure, that is, the two words are said to have the same meaning. It can be represented this way:

1 good = df pleasure

It is important for us to ask whether or not pleasure is good so that we may know whether we should devote ourselves to the pursuit of pleasure or whether there may not be other goals that are more worthy. Thus we ask:

2 Is pleasure good?

Now take the definition of "good" stated in 1 and substitute it for the word "good" in 2. The question then becomes:

3 Is pleasure pleasure?

We could also make the substitution the other way and then we have:

4 Is good good?

Both 3 and 4 are trivialities and not at all the question that we wanted to ask about pleasure. The conclusion of the argument is that the definition 1 does not capture what we mean by the word "good."

The argument can be generalized and used to object to any definition of good. Let "A" represent any word or expression that is offered as a definition of good:

1′ good = df A

We then ask:

2′ Is A good?

Substituting from 1′ we get:

3′ Is A, A? (or: Is good good?)

What we wanted to be an important question evaporates into a triviality. No definition, it is claimed, can capture for us what the word "good" means. It should be obvious that the same form of argument can also be used to criticize any attempted definition of what is morally right.

We are now in a position to understand how the argument applies to theological ethics. We begin with the definition:

1″ right = df what God wills

We then ask

2″ Does God will what is right?

By the definition 1″ the question becomes the trivial

3″ Does God will what God wills?

Most religious people would certainly want to say that God in fact wills what is right and that is an important thing to know about God. If we accept the definition that what is right is simply what God wills, then it becomes logically impossible to praise God for His justice and righteousness; we can only say that He wills what He wills.

We might think about the problem with theological ethics by asking this question. With respect to morality is God an absolute or a constitutional monarch? The word of the absolute monarch is law and it makes no sense to wonder whether such a king could issue an illegal decree. This opens the possibility that the king's will could be altogether arbitrary and his commands no more than the expression of his whims. His decrees, be what they may, are, by the very definition of absolutism, the law. The situation of the constitutional monarch, however, is different. His decrees can be judged in accordance with the constitution which is a body of law existing in logical independence of the will of the king and against which the will of the king can be judged. In the case of the constitutional monarch it makes sense to question whether some decree is constitutional and therefore has the force of law. The wise constitutional monarch is he who governs with his eyes firmly fixed on the law which furnishes him both reason and justification for his decrees.

If we think of God as the absolute moral monarch, then it is hard to escape the conclusion that His will is arbitrary and that there are no logical grounds for attributing to Him goodness, mercy, or justice. How, then, could we understand the words of, say, Psalm 19?

> The law of the LORD is perfect / the testimony of the LORD is sure / the precepts of the LORD are right / the commandment of the LORD is pure / the ordinances of the LORD are true and righteous altogether.

If God is the absolute moral monarch, then all such praises reduce to the tautology that His will is His will and believers can only prostrate themselves before the arbitrary power of God.

There are a host of other familiar problems with theological ethics. If it is true, then there would then seem to be no grounds for the ethical condemnation of the murderer and no way to distinguish between the bloody commandments of Yahweh in the early scriptures and the injunctions of the Sermon on the Mount. We seem driven to conclude that there must be a standard or criterion of moral goodness that can be known independently of the will of God and in terms of which we praise God and find his commandments worthy of being obeyed, but we have no idea what this independent standard of morality is, what its origins are, nor how we ought to go about discovering it.

The logical landscape of theological ethics that we have just surveyed presents the religious believer with a problem. The believer wants to say that God is the source and authority of all morality, yet a consistent adherence to that article of faith leads to all the difficulties and contradictions we have just seen. This is a philosophical problem and as a philosophical problem it has an interesting characteristic. You may be pulled in the direction of wanting to think of God as the ultimate moral authority, but at the same time you can be pulled in another direction by the arguments we have been considering. This may produce a feeling of intellectual, if not moral and religious, confusion; it is as if you do not know your way about. This sense of being pulled in two directions is the mark of a serious person recognizing a serious philosophical problem. It is a position from which an individual will have to struggle to escape.

We cannot here offer a solution to this problem. Although there may be one, an investigation of it is well beyond the scope of this little book. In the meanwhile here are a couple of points to be kept in mind while you are thinking about it. We said at the beginning of the chapter that what scripture represents as the commands of God is not complete in that these commands do not speak to every possible moral situation. As a matter of fact, no moral code can do that. We must see why.

The law and/or the teachings of Jesus can be thought of as rules telling us to do this or not to do that. Rules, all rules, have to be applied. The rule "You shall not murder" seems clear enough, but, as we saw, there can be serious questions about what is and what is not a case of murder. The rule has to be applied to particular cases, but there is no rule for applying the rule. At some point we must decide that the rule applies to this case, but not to that other one, and so on. There is not another rule to guide us in this decision. There comes a time when we simply have to go ahead and act without any further guidance. A first step in resolving our problem, consequently, may require us to look very carefully at how religious people actually make use of the appeal to the word of God as a guide to the conduct of their lives.

There is an interesting example of this kind of use in Judaism. The Jews had long realized that the Mosaic law was unclear on some points and that it said nothing about problems that cropped up in later centuries. For people who took the law seriously and who lived by the law there was a great practical need for interpretation and application. As a result there developed a tradition within Judaism of interpreting the law and applying it to particular situations and of modifying it to meet changing conditions of life. This tradition was already old by the time of Christ in the first century of our era.[6]

There is also another kind of example worth noting. King David had coveted Bathsheba who was another man's wife. He took her for himself and arranged that her husband be killed in battle. The prophet Nathan came to David and told him the story of a poor man whose only possession was a ewe lamb that he had raised and loved like a daughter. A rich and powerful man, too mean to slaughter one of his own sheep, took the poor man's lamb for a feast. David was outraged at this injustice and demanded that the man be identified and punished. Nathan replied, "Thou art the man!" (II Samuel 12:7).[7] This case makes clear that the awareness that there are rules against theft and adultery is not by itself enough; one also has to be able to recognize the nature of one's own deeds and how they fall under the rules. David did not make the connection between the commandments and his own deeds until Nathan's story brought it home to him.

It is an important feature of morality that its duties and obligations can appear to make absolute and unqualified demands upon a person. Moral duties are not like our own personal whims and desires that can be acted on or ignored as the mood strikes us and they seem to have an authority that far outstrips that of social customs, conventions, and pressures or even of any legal system. It has seemed to many thinkers that the values and demands of morality are built into the very fabric of the world itself.

This view of morality has suggested an argument for the existence of God, the so-called moral argument that we mentioned in chapter 2. The widely read Christian author C. S. Lewis has proposed such an argument. Morality, he argues, is not any human contrivance, but an objective law of the universe. The best explanation of the existence of this law is a creating mind, i.e. God, that bids us do our moral duty.[8]

This argument has obvious similarities to the argument from design and like that argument can be understood as an inference from the way some people think about morality to what they believe to be the only possible, or at least reasonable, explanation. For the argument to begin to be convincing, however, it would have to show that there is no other satisfactory explanation of the nature of morality and that has not yet been done. The argument is probably best thought of not as an argument at all, but rather as an expression of the religious belief in God as Lawgiver.

The Problem of Evil

We want to turn now to the second of the philosophical tasks mentioned at the beginning of the chapter about explaining the existence of evil. The traditional problem about evil in the world can be stated very simply. Consider the following four propositions.

1 God is omnipotent (He is all-powerful).
2 God is omniscient (He is all-knowing).
3 God is infinitely benevolent (He desires only good).
4 Evil exists.

The problem arises from the claim that these propositions are logically inconsistent, that is, they cannot all be true. If evil exists, then we must consider these possibilities: (a) God is unable to prevent it; (b) God does not know how to prevent it; or (c) He does not wish to prevent it. Possibility (a) contradicts proposition 1 about God's omnipotence; (b) contradicts proposition 2 about His omniscience; and (c) contradicts proposition 3 about His benevolence.[9]

One way to avoid the inconsistencies is to deny one or more of the traditional attributes of God stated in propositions 1, 2, and 3. Thus God may be very powerful, but not all that powerful; He may know a great deal, but not all that much; or there may be a bit of a mean streak in Him. The ancient religion of Persia, Zoroastrianism, denied the omnipotence of God. It postulated two gods, Ahura Mazda, god of goodness and light, and Ahriman, god of darkness and evil. It thought of the world as a battleground between the forces of good and evil although in his fight against evil, it was believed, Ahura Mazda would ultimately be victorious.[10]

That God may not be altogether benevolent has been expressed many times. In his poem "Caliban upon Setebos" (1864) Robert Browning recounts Caliban's[11] meditation upon Setebos, the god worshipped by his mother. Caliban says, "He is strong and Lord./ 'Am strong myself compared to yonder crabs / That march now from the mountain to the sea; / 'Let twenty pass and stone the twenty-first, / . . . As it likes me each time I do: so He."

To suppose that God is not altogether benevolent is to reject the conception of God that has come to characterize developed monotheism and serious religious thinkers have not wanted to do that. The more usual course is to stick to the traditional conception of God and then to try to find a means of explaining the existence of evil in such a way that it turns out not to be God's doing.

One of the most influential attempts to deal with the problem was made by St Augustine.[12] As a Christian thinker Augustine has to claim that the world is God's creation and since it derives from God it can only be good; evil cannot come from God. He then suggests that evil is the result of human choice. We have free will and too often choose to do evil rather than good. He immediately sees a problem with this. God created us and created us with a will capable of making the wrong choices; therefore it appears that God is, after all, responsible for evil.

To understand how he tries to resolve this problem we have to understand something of Augustine's general philosophical theory. As we noted in chapter 3 this is a metaphysical theory derived from the Neo-Platonism of Plotinus. In Augustine's version of this metaphysics God created everything and everything that exists is good. There is in this scheme an identity between goodness and existence so that if something is deprived of goodness it will not exist at all. Although everything is good, some things are better than others, that is, they possess more goodness. Thus there is a hierarchy, an order, of goodness and a corresponding hierarchy of existence. The things that stand closest to God have more goodness and more existence than those that are farther from God. It follows from this picture of the world that evil is not a substance, that is to say, it is not a thing. If it were a thing, then it would be good. Since evil is not a thing, it is not something that God created; God cannot be blamed for the existence of evil and is thus taken off the hook.

To learn that evil is not a substance is not yet to know what it is. Augustine tells us that evil is a perversion of the will when it turns aside from God and higher things and veers towards things of the lowest order. He makes the curious statement that for God evil does not exist and then goes on to say that we think of things as evil because they are at variance with other things. He gives the example of bad weather. It may be at variance with our interests and so we think of it as bad, but it is appropriate to the earth. The implication of this is that our judgment that something is evil is the result of a limited perspective. If we had a comprehensive view of things we would realize that everything has its appropriate place and we would come to understand that, although the higher things are better than the lower things, the totality of creation is better than the higher things alone.

There are several things about this view of Augustine's that we must examine. To do this it will be useful to recall our understanding of philosophy as conceptual investigation. We are here concerned with the *concept* of evil and we examine a concept by looking at how the relevant word is used and understood. When Augustine says that we think of some things as evil we can understand him to mean that we use the word "evil" to describe various situations, people, and their actions. Examples are not wanting. There are the natural evils of floods, earthquakes, volcanic eruptions, and the like, that cause immense human suffering. There are also the moral evils that result from the evil actions of evil people such as wars, rape, and torture that are all too familiar to us. We have, unfortunately, plenty of examples that we can use in order to explain and teach the meaning and application of the word "evil," the Nazi atrocities during the Hitler era, the behavior of the warring factions in Bosnia or the Sudan, or a hundred more.

There is more, remember, to our understanding of the concept of evil that simply being able to apply the word in various circumstances. Our concepts and our language are grounded in our lives and practices. We react to evil deeds with horror, we try to prevent them, we seek to punish those who do evil, we seek to solace and comfort the victims of the torturer and the victims of natural disasters. The application of the word thus has far-reaching consequences.

Augustine, however, says that evil does not exist for God. This implies that there is nothing to which God applies the word "evil." Were we to meet one of those situations that we could use as an example for teaching the word and say "This is evil," we must imagine God replying, "No, it's not." What are we to make of this? How could anyone, including God, deny that this is evil? If He denies it is evil, then the fact that these people were victims of the evil would not be a reason for God to comfort them. Nor could He have any reason to prevent people from doing evil.

We may be forced to conclude that God does not speak our language. If the word "evil" means anything to Him, it cannot mean what it means to us. Like so many other words in our language, "evil" and "good" go together. We must understand them by the contrasts they mark. So if God does not mean by "evil" what we mean, then he cannot mean by "good" what we mean either. It becomes impossible to understand what Augustine is trying to tell us about God and good and evil.

The attempt to explain why God permits evil to exist is really an attempt to show that God is *justified* in arranging things as He did and not just being careless or cruel. Such an attempt is called a *theodicy*; a theodicy, then, as John Milton put it in *Paradise Lost* (1667), seeks "to justify the ways of God to men." The English poet A. E. Housman apparently thought little of theodicy when he wrote that "malt does more than Milton can / To justify the ways of God to man."[13]

An especially interesting theodicy was produced by the German philosopher and mathematician G. W. Leibniz (1646–1716). Leibniz was a contemporary of Isaac Newton. Both Leibniz and Newton developed the integral and differential calculus although they worked quite independently of one another.[14] Arguing as a mathematician and logician, Leibniz said that, when it came to creating the world, God had to choose from an infinite number of possible worlds. The one he chose to actualize was, naturally, the best of all possible worlds. Leibniz's work has intrigued philosophers in the twentieth century largely because of his logical interests that tended to anticipate more modern developments. Logicians, we may add, have been very much enamored during the past several decades of the concept of possible worlds. Even the best of all possible worlds, however, contains features that strike us as evil.

Leibniz's concept of the best of all possible worlds has been delightfully parodied by Voltaire in his wonderful little novel *Candide* (1759). Candide is, as his name suggests, a naive young chap who has been tutored by Dr Pangloss in a philosophy reminiscent of Leibniz's. After being forcibly conscripted into the army he was forced to run the regimental gauntlet 36 times – which laid bare the muscles and nerves from his neck to his backside. About the same time his lady love, Mlle Cunegonde, was raped to the limit of possibility by Bulgarian soldiers and then disemboweled. Be assured, however, that they survived those ordeals and went on to experience further misfortunes. No matter what happened they were reassured by Dr Pangloss that it was all for the best in this the best of all possible worlds.

Leibniz's kind of theodicy implies that evil is necessary to produce a world that is on the whole good. Voltaire ridiculed the idea with parody, but Fyodor Dostoyevsky describes an objection to it that arises from the deepest moral outrage. In his novel *The Brothers Karamazov* (1880) Ivan, the intellectual brother, talks about these things with his younger brother, Alyosha, who is studying for the priesthood. Ivan longs for a world of love, reconciliation and harmony in which sins are atoned for. He goes on to describe horrible abuses that people inflict upon children and claims that the suffering of innocent children can never be atoned for. If this suffering is necessary to achieve that harmony, then, says Ivan, he wants his entrance ticket back. He does not deny the existence of God, but he wants no part of God's plan if that plan demands the torture of children.[15]

We have presented the problem of evil as a theoretical problem, a problem about whether four propositions are logically consistent. It is highly doubtful, however, that the problem of evil has a satisfactory theoretical or intellectual solution. The Augustinian and Leibnizian solutions ask us to accept complex philosophical and metaphysical schemes whose intelligibility is very much in question. Milton's *Paradise Lost* is surely one of the great works of English literature, but we must keep in mind that it is essentially a work of imaginative fiction that draws on both scriptural and Christian folklore and cannot play the role of either explanation or justification of God's ways.

The aim of theodicy is to *justify* the ways of God to man. Let us note the oddness, the conceptual oddness, of seeking to justify God's purposes and actions. A man or a woman can be called upon to justify his or her actions. To justify one's actions is to show that they were, in fact, in accord with accepted moral principles or were intended, appearances notwithstanding, to achieve some desirable result. Justification, then, as we understand it takes place against a background of accepted principles and practices and these must be our own principles and practices. In the absence of such a background there is nothing that can be called justification. If we are to justify the ways of God, then we have no choice but to do so in terms of our own principles and practices.

It is doubtful, however, that this makes any sense. God is not just another actor in the human drama to be judged as we judge other people and, as we saw in the first part of this chapter, we know of no moral code logically independent of the will of God against which God Himself can be judged and justified. There is a concept of God according to which any attempt to question or judge God is out of place.

Consider the book of Job. Job was a righteous and blameless man who obeyed the law of Moses in all particulars. God had promised that those who obeyed the law would be blessed and would prosper.[16] That is a premise of the story. The first two chapters describe a council of the Divine Beings in which God boasts of His servant Job. The Adversary[17] claims that he can make Job blaspheme against God and God gives him leave to try to do so. The Adversary then visits a dreadful series of misfortunes upon Job. The remainder of the book, however, says no more about the arrangement between God and the Adversary.[18]

Job eventually wants to know why he should suffer when he has been righteous. The answer that he finally gets from God is in one sense no answer at all. God tells him that he has no knowledge of divine ways and is in no position to put any questions to God. At one point God says, "Would you impugn My justice? / Would you condemn Me that you may be right?" (40:8). In another sense, however, this may be exactly the answer that is wanted.

God's response may suggest to many that it is impious to try to bring God to account, but let us seek to understand it in another way. To think of it as impious is to suppose that there is something to be done that can be intelligibly described; it is just that it should not be done. Suppose, by contrast, that we take God's response to be calling our attention to the conceptual point that it makes no sense to impugn His justice, to call Him to account for his actions, or to seek to justify His ways. Taken in that way we see that it is not intelligible to ask for a justification of God's ways. Job was humbled by God's response to him and from a certain philosophical point of view we can recognize that humiliation to include his attempt to extend his language beyond the limits of intelligibility.

The real problem of evil, let us suggest, is not theoretical, but is the practical problem of how one lives a religious life in a world of evil and misfortune, a life that includes, among other things, worship, prayer, and faith in God. One example of such a life is shown by Dietrich Bonhoeffer (1906–45). Bonhoeffer was a prominent German Lutheran pastor and theologian who was accused of plotting against Hitler. He was arrested by the Nazis and after a year in prison was hung by the Gestapo in April of 1945. It is in his life and writings while in prison, a time when he did not know from one day to the next what would happen to him, that we have an illustration of one kind of response to the evil in the world.

When Bonhoeffer was faced with the evil in the world and his own suffering of it, he did not react by raising the traditional problem of evil or ask why God should permit it. He does say that God brings good out of evil, but there is nothing in his remark to suggest that some theoretical explanation is in order to account for how such a transmutation can take place. What he means can best be understood as an expression of a resolve to go on living and working in the eventual hope that things will turn out and that one will grow spiritually through the trials of life. His suffering is never considered a challenge to his faith, rather it is his religious faith that allows him to meet the challenge of suffering, He says, "The consciousness of being borne up by a spiritual tradition that goes back for centuries gives one a feeling of confidence and security in the face of all passing strains and stresses."[19]

For some, however, it is not possible to live a religious life in a world of suffering and evil. During the Second World War the Nazis in Germany undertook the systematic destruction of the Jews of Europe. They actually succeeded in killing some five or six million Jews in the concentration camps with their gas chambers and cremating ovens by what came to be almost production-line methods.[20] The conditions of Bonhoeffer's imprisonment were bad enough, but were not altogether lacking in human amenities. He had books to read, could write and receive letters, and had occasional visitors. By contrast, the conditions in the death camps were beyond description. Jews reacted to these conditions in a number of different ways.

Like Bonhoeffer, many Jews relied on their faith to see them through the ordeal and did what they could to maintain their religious traditions and practices under the most trying conditions. Others thought of what was happening as God's punishment for their sins or imagined God to have abandoned them.[21] The influential Jewish writer Elie Wiesel expresses this sense of abandonment in a passage in which he describes the hanging of three inmates of a concentration camp accused of sabotage. Two of them were adults and the other a child. The inmates were paraded to watch the execution. "Where is God?" one of them asked as the hanging began. Wiesel goes on to relate the affair.

> The two adults were no longer alive. Their tongues hung swollen, blue-tinged. But the third rope was still moving; being so light, the child was still alive . . . For more than half an hour he stayed there, struggling between life and

> death, dying a slow agony under our eyes. And we had to look him full in the face. He was still alive when I passed in front of him. His tongue was still red, his eyes were not yet glazed. Behind me, I heard the same man asking: "Where is God now?" And I heard a voice within me answer him: "Where is He? Here He is – He is hanging here on this gallows. . . ." That night the soup tasted of corpses.[22]

If there is a conclusion to be reached about the problem of evil, it is that the theoretical problem with which we began about whether or not four propositions are logically consistent is only the palest reflection of the struggles of life.

Suggestions for Further Reading

Theological ethics

Standard objections to theological ethics are found in Richard Price, *A Review of the Principal Questions in Morals* (Oxford: Clarendon Press, 1948), ch. 1, sect. 1, first published in 1758, and in Moritz Schlick, *Problems of Ethics* (New York: Dover Publications, 1962), originally published in 1930. A suggestive criticism of Schlick's objection is offered by Ludwig Wittgenstein in Brian McGuinness, ed., *Wittgenstein and the Vienna Circle* (Oxford: Basil Blackwell, 1979), p. 115.

The problem of evil

John Hick's *Evil and the Love of God* (New York: Harper & Row, 1966) is a useful and detailed survey of the various approaches to the problem of evil. Edward H. Madden and Peter H. Hare, *Evil and the Concept of God* (Springfield, Ill.: Charles C. Thomas Publisher, 1968), is an interesting examination of the problem from the point of view of recent Anglo-American analytical philosophy.

For Jewish religious reaction to the Holocaust see R. L. Rubenstein, *After Auschwitz: Radical Theology and Contemporary Judaism* (Indianapolis: Bobbs-Merrill, 1966).

Notes

1 The word "ethics" is derived from the Greek *ethos* and "morality" is from the Latin *mores*. The Greek and the Latin words both refer to the customs of a people. As English words the two are essentially synonomous.
2 There are two versions of the so-called Ten Commandments, Genesis 20 and Deuteronomy 5.
3 The Mosaic distinction between clean and unclean flesh has nothing to do with health and sanitation, but is purely a ritual distinction.
4 Richard Price, *A Review of the Principal Questions in Morals* (Oxford: Clarendon Press, 1948), pp. 16–17. (First published in 1758.)
5 G. E. Moore, *Principia Ethica* (Cambridge: Cambridge University Press, 1954), p. 15. (First published 1903.)
6 The traditional interpretations and applications of the law are contained in the collection known as the Talmud. It was largely the work of the Pharisees and Scribes (interpreters), the liberal faction of Judaism that developed the institution of the synagogue and the rabbi.
7 The Jewish Bible translation that we have been using has "That man is you!" but the traditional King James rendering is dramatically more effective.
8 This argument is found in C. S. Lewis, *Mere Christianity*, revised and enlarged edn (New York: Macmillan, 1978). In his *Critique of Pure Reason* of 1788 Immanuel Kant argued for a connection between an objective moral law and the existence of God. Kant, however, did not use the notion of moral law as a premise in an argument for the existence of

God, but argued instead that the existence of God, along with human freedom and the immortality of the soul, is a necessary *postulate* required to make sense of our moral concepts.

9 David Hume states a version of this problem in *Dialogues Concerning Natural Religion*, Part X. Hume attributes the problem to Epicurus, but its origin is obscure.

10 Zoroastrianism is named for its founder Zoroaster (sometimes "Zarathustra") who lived from the late seventh century to the middle of the sixth century BC. The idea of Ahriman, the god of evil and darkness, had considerable influence on the later Judaic concept of Satan and the devil.

11 Caliban is the monster in Shakespeare's play *The Tempest*

12 This account of St Augustine's position is taken from his *Confessions*, Book VII.

13 From the poem "Terence, This is Stupid Stuff . . ." It can be found in his collection, *A Shropshire Lad* (1896).

14 The modern symbolism of the calculus is based on Leibniz's rather than Newton's original notation.

15 This conversation occurs in Part II, Book V, ch. V, "Rebellion."

16 See Deuteronomy 7, for example.

17 "The Adversary," in Hebrew "the Satan." The reader must remember that the character in this story is not the devil of later folklore.

18 The first two chapters are written in prose while the rest of the book is poetry. That, together with the fact that the council in heaven is heard no more of, makes clear that the book is an amalgam of two different tales.

19 Dietrich Bonhoeffer, *Letters and Papers from Prison*, enlarged edition, ed. Eberhard Bethge (New York: Macmillan, 1971), p. 165.

20 This destruction of the Jews has come to be known as the Holocaust. The word is derived from the Greek and refers to a burnt sacrifice or something completed destroyed by fire.

21 The various religious reactions to the Holocaust are catalogued by Paul Marcus and Alan Rosenberg in their article "Faith, Ethics and the Holocaust," in *Holocaust and Genocide Studies*, vol. 3, no. 4 (1988).

22 Elie Wiesel, *Night* (New York: Hill & Wang, 1960), pp. 70–1.

6

Religion, Life, and Philosophy

The Rational Challenge to Religion

It is time now to tie up some of the loose ends that were left dangling in the earlier chapters and to reach some conclusions, however tentative, about religion and the philosophical problems that have surrounded it. Those dangling ends were sometimes the consequences of the largely negative results that our philosophical inquiries have tended toward so far. We have seen that the traditional arguments for the existence of God won't work, that the Bible cannot be understood as an historical record either of God's activity in the world or of the life of Jesus, that there can be no historical or empirical evidence for miracles, and that there are grave difficulties in trying to understand our ethical and moral standards as based on the will of God. In a word, what all this suggests is that our religious beliefs cannot be given any rational justification by logical argument, empirical science, or historical investigation. Let us pursue the consequences of this suggestion.

There are many people who will believe things in the absence of any evidence or justification; they will believe what they read in the tabloids about Elvis still being alive or aliens from outer space moving among us. Such people are naive, credulous, gullible, or just plain stupid. If there is no evidence or other rational justification for religious belief, then it can appear that the religious believer is also open to the charge of being naive, credulous, gullible, or just plain stupid. And this is precisely the charge that is sometimes leveled against the believer.

This charge against the believer implies that religious beliefs are either false or at least not known to be true. The former is the position of the atheist who denies the existence of God. The latter is the position of the agnostic[1] who claims that we do not have sufficient information to allow us to decide anything about the existence of God.

There are, however, more radical and deeper challenges to religious belief than the claim that it is simply false. One such challenge came from a group of philosophers and scientists in Vienna in the 1920s that was known as the Vienna Circle. Out of the discussions of this group developed the philosophical movement of logical positivism. From their reflections on the nature of philosophy, science, and mathematics they arrived at a theory about the meaning of the words and sentences of our language. A sentence is said to be meaningful if, and only if, it is a sentence in a logical or mathematical system or is at least in principle capable of having its truth or falsity determined by empirical observations. If a sentence does not satisfy either of these conditions, then it is literally meaningless, that is, nonsense.

One of the aims of this theory of meaning was to distinguish the propositions and theories of genuine empirical science from the pretensions of philosophical metaphysics to describe what the world is really like. Since metaphysical theories can be neither confirmed nor disconfirmed in experience, they were dismissed as nonsense. The implications of the theory for religious beliefs, e.g. statements about God, is obvious and they were drawn explicitly by the English philosopher A. J. Ayer (1910–89), who became very interested in logical positivism.[2]

Ayer points out that statements about God neither are verifiable in experience nor belong to any logical or mathematical system. They are, therefore, nonsense. This allows him to put an interesting twist on the traditional religious positions of theism, atheism, and agnosticism. Theism claims that God exists, atheism denies that God exists, while agnosticism says that God either exists or doesn't, but that we do not have the knowledge that would permit us to come down on one side of the question or the other. We tend to think of these three positions as dividing up the territory. Ayer says that the three can be characterized by their stance to the truth value of the sentence "God exists." The theist says it is true, the atheist says it is false, and the agnostic says it is either true or false, but we don't know which. They all three agree that the sentence has a truth value and that implies they all believe the sentence is meaningful, that it makes sense. If, as Ayer and the positivists claim, the sentence is meaningless, then it has no truth value and the three traditional positions are meaningless. Ayer is neither a theist, nor an atheist, nor an agnostic! Religious believers now have to defend their position, not merely against the charge that it is false, but against the more serious charge that it makes no sense.

It is now well understood that the theory of meaning associated with logical positivism is inadequate, but that is not sufficient for religion to claim that its beliefs are therefore meaningful. For all its shortcomings positivism did call attention to something important about our language. If we are going to set out to make statements about the world, to describe things, we must be prepared to say how our statements could be shown to be either true or false. If someone told us that he had been raised by the Apache Indians we could check his story through newspaper accounts, talking to the Apaches, and other familiar methods of inquiry. But when Pogo tells us of being raised by a tribe of invisible Indians there is, of course, no conceivable way to verify what he says and it begins to look suspiciously like a piece of nonsense.[3]

Religious beliefs have the appearance of statements about the world, but we know of nothing that could either confirm or deny them. This opens the way to supposing that talk about our relations with God is not really different from talk about our relations with invisible Indians. Even if the positivist theory of meaning does not give us a justification for saying that religious beliefs are out-and-out nonsense, those beliefs can still appear very suspicious.

Before we dismiss religious beliefs as without rational foundation or, even worse, as nonsense and religious believers as naive and uncritical, let's take another look at religious belief. A religious man says, for example, that God will forgive sins. Let us also suppose that he says that under certain conditions his boss will forgive a worker's mistake. When asked how he knows this he can reply that it is the boss's announced policy and that he has seen him do so on a number of occasions. He cannot, of course, do anything like that with God and the forgiveness of sins.

What he can do, and what is usually done when that question arises, is to support the claim by citing appropriate passages from the Bible.

At this point it seems in order to raise the obvious objection that there are no grounds for regarding the Bible as the announced policy of God since there is no independent way to know that the Bible comes from God as we know that the company policy comes from the boss's desk. To assume it does is to beg all the questions at issue. What can actually happen, however, is that the religious person may simply reject the demand to justify the Bible. That is very unlike what he does in the case of the boss and in so many other daily affairs. He can check the boss's behavior against the announced policy and can even be prepared to revise his views about the boss's consistency and mercy.

The purpose of what we have just said is to show how differently statements of religious belief are treated from statements and conjectures that figure in other aspects of our lives such as scholarly and scientific endeavors, not to mention ordinary day-to-day matters. The question that faces us is what to make of this difference.

One possibility is to say simply that when it comes to religion people leave at the door of the synagogue or church the common sense and critical intelligence that serve them well in the rest of their lives. This is a clear implication of the position we described earlier that takes religious statements to pretend to the status of ordinary statements but not to measure up to that status.

Rudolf Bultmann and the Mythological View of the World

Another kind of challenge to the religious believer came from Rudolf Bultmann (1884–1976), one of the most influential Biblical scholars and theologians of the first half of the twentieth century. He wrote from the perspective of one who is aware of and at home in modern ways of thinking about the world and at the same time is a deeply committed Christian. From this perspective he describes a problem that intellectually honest Christians must face.

Christians, of course, accept the New Testament as the basis of their faith and it was largely from New Testament materials that later Christian doctrine was formulated.[4] Bultmann makes clear to us by means of many scriptural references what the cosmology of the New Testament was like, that is, how the world was pictured and understood by people in the cultural context that produced the New Testament.[5] He describes this cosmology as mythical. He describes it as a "three-storied" structure. The earth is flat, heaven is above it, and hell beneath it. It is in terms of this cosmology that we must understand the accounts of Christ *descending* into hell and *ascending* into heaven. The angels of God and the demons of Satan are everywhere at work in the world. Men can be possessed by demons or they can be inspired by God and granted visions. This world will soon come to an end in some sort of catastrophe, the dead will be raised, there will be a final judgment which will grant eternal salvation to some and subject others to eternal damnation. These events will be ushered in by the coming of Christ, the pre-existent Word of God, whose death, resurrection, and ascension to sit on the right hand of God will be the crucial events in the eschatological[6] drama. This picture of the physical layout of the world, we should note, has none of the scientific sophistication of the Greek physics and astronomy contemporary with it and the Greeks would never have populated their world with angels and demons. The Jews, after all, had never been involved with science at any time in their history.

Bultmann very frankly points out that in our own time it is impossible for us to accept this mythical cosmology. The development of astronomy and physics, not to mention the other sciences, from the seventeenth century on govern our view of the world. We cannot honestly think of heaven as above our heads and hell as beneath our feet. Nor can we conceive of the world as populated by demons or as coming to an end at any time now.

Bultmann's description of New Testament cosmology is absolutely correct as a careful reading of the text will show. We have already seen how religious views and doctrines can be quite out of reach of any kind of empirical or rational investigation, whether of logic, science, or history. Some religious believers have seen in this a challenge to their belief. Bultmann's work presents a challenge of a rather different, although related, kind. The doctrines of the faith are framed in terms of a world view that we cannot understand. It is not just that there is no empirical evidence of Christ's ascension into heaven, it is rather that there is no *place* above the earth for Christ to ascend to. To rise from the earth is simply to go out into what is very possibly infinite space. Our modern view of the world augmented in the years after Bultmann's death forces us to imagine the ascension as like the space shuttle taking off and keeping on going to who knows where. This clearly won't do if for no other reason than that it replaces something of religious significance with a feat of physics.

Bultmann thinks that in order to save Christian belief the New Testament must be *demythologized*, that is, the mythological elements must be stripped away to reveal the essential message beneath it. This essential message is called by the Greek word *kerygma* which has become a term of art within theology. The key to the project of demythologizing is the understanding of myth. Bultmann says that

> The real point of myth is not to give an objective world picture; what is expressed in it, rather, is how we human beings understand ourselves in the world. Thus, myth does not want to be interpreted in cosmological terms but in anthropological terms – or, better, in existentialist terms.[7]

This passage tells us that we should not think of the New Testament view of the world as in any way pretending to scientific status, but instead as a way of saying something very important about human life. The word "existentialist" reveals Bultmann's debt to the philosophical movement known as existentialism associated with such thinkers as Karl Jaspars and Martin Heidegger in Germany and Jean-Paul Sartre in France. The appeal to existentialism is possibly unfortunate, since that philosophy may be thought to darken counsel more than to enlighten, but, for all that, its importance lies in its focus on problems that people face in living in the world.

The point of Bultmann's project of demythologizing is brought out in what he says about Christ:

> the salvation occurrence about which we talk is not some miraculous, supernatural occurrence but rather a historical occurrence in space and time. And by presenting it as such, stripping away the mythological garments, we have

> intended to follow the New Testament itself and to do full justice to the paradox of its proclamation – the paradox, namely, that God's eschatological emissary is a concrete historical person, that God's eschatological act takes place in a human destiny, that it is an occurrence, therefore, that cannot be proved to be eschatological in any worldly way.[8]

In this passage Bultmann is telling us that when all the mythological trappings of the cosmic drama are stripped away we are left with the knowledge that Jesus was a real person whose execution by crucifixion was an historical fact. There is, however, a paradox in this fact. It is of the greatest eschatological (i.e. religious) significance, yet that significance cannot be shown by any worldly means, that is, no historical inquiry or scientific marshalling of evidence can show it. We have already been at pains to make clear that there is this kind of logical gap between historical fact and religious significance. Bultmann will go on to say that to understand Jesus as the Christ whose death brings salvation and a new life requires faith.

Bultmann's appeal to existentialism may be baggage that can be left behind, but it does point us in a direction where it may be useful to look, namely that the important thing about religion lies in *how* one looks at the facts of the world – the same facts that the non-believer acknowledges – and how that way of looking at things enters one's life.

Believing that God Exists and Believing in God

What we have just seen of Bultmann's work can suggest to us another possibility that we want to explore although it is not one that is explicit in anything he says. It is that religious beliefs are very different in kind from both scientific and everyday beliefs about the world. They play a very different role in the lives of people. They are not subject to standards of evidence or to possible revision as other beliefs are. They condition a person's stance to his or her own life, to other people, and to the whole world in a way that other beliefs do not. Much misunderstanding of religion is the result of supposing that to be religious is largely a matter of believing that certain *propositions* are true, propositions whose only difference from other kinds of propositions is that they are about supernatural rather than natural facts. This misunderstanding is exhibited from both outside and inside religion. It leads the religious outsider, the non-believer, to dismiss religion and religious people as foolish. It has led some religious people to try to support their beliefs with arguments and evidence, but, since the arguments are invariably bad and the "evidence" cannot stand up to scholarly and scientific standards, they end up making themselves foolish.

The first step toward getting a better understanding of what religion may be is to turn our attention away from thinking of religious belief as mostly a matter of holding certain propositions to be true to thinking of religion as a way of living. Let's return to the question that has been occupying us since the second chapter: Does God exist? It is worth reminding ourselves that the proposition "There is a God" does not appear in any religious creed. The Christian Apostle's Creed says, "I believe *in* God the Father Almighty . . ." and not "I believe that there is a God." What does it mean to believe *in* something?

The bank president may say, "I believe in that young Smurthwaite," and a diplomat may announce that he believes in the United Nations. The bank president's remark tells us that he believes Smurthwaite to be a responsible and enterprising lad and more than likely expresses the president's willingness to lend Smurthwaite the money to build the factory to manufacture his newly invented steam-powered computer. To believe in the United Nations is to support its policies, to cooperate in its projects, to accept the results of its arbitrations, and the like.

These examples of "believing in" are only of limited help in understanding what it is to believe in God. To be sure, religious people believe in God in the sense that they trust Him and rely on His promises. There must, however, be more to it than that. One might object here that, in order to believe in young Smurthwaite, the bank president must already know, or at least believe, that there really is a young Smurthwaite and the diplomat must already know that there is such an organization as the United Nations in order to support its policies. Likewise, it may be thought, in order to believe in and trust God one must begin by believing that there really is a God. And so we seem to be brought right back to the question that we set aside.

We need to back up a step. Paradoxical as it may seem, in order to believe in God we do not first have to establish that God exists. There may not be anything at all that can be called "establishing that God exists." Religious belief or, to use another word, faith is in this respect different from the other examples of "believing in." We can get some sense of this difference by recalling what we said at the beginning of chapter 2 about arguments and reasons for believing that God exists.

Some of the reasons we listed for why people say they believe God exists were that the Bible says so, the existence and complexity of the world, the fact of miracles, how belief has changed a life, and that one has been taught to believe. When we tried to make these reasons into premises of deductive arguments or as evidence toward inductive conclusions, the results, we saw, were hopeless. Nevertheless, it was said that these reasons all had a religious importance. Now it is time to try to make clear what that importance is.

Let us start with the existence and complexity of the world. We originally took this as a kind of first approximation of Cleanthes' argument from design and we have learned that argument is a bad one. But we do not have to take it as part of an argument or as evidence for the existence of God. Psalm 19 says, "The heavens declare the glory of God, / the sky proclaims His handiwork." Note that the psalmist did not say that the heavens are *evidence* for the existence of God. A person can be impressed with the world and with its workings. This can take the form of seeing the starry heavens, for example, as the handiwork of God or even of seeing God in all of that. One does not have to think of God and His glory as something that lies behind the starry heavens and for which the heavens are only evidence any more than one has to think of the smile on the face of a child on Christmas morning as evidence of her delight. The delight is not something lurking behind the smile; it is declared right in the smile.

The important thing to keep in mind here is that one can react to the world in this way. To react to the world by seeing it as the handiwork of God is already to take a religious stance. The argument from design exploits this kind of reaction, but misrepresents it. It misrepresents it by treating what the religious person sees in the world as evidence when it would have been wiser and closer to a genuine religious outlook to understand the reaction as an expression or manifestation of religious belief.

An analogy – which is by no means a perfect one – may help to explain what we have been saying. We look at the clouds in the sky. They may appear as formless shapes or random clusters. After a bit some of them may take on an organization and pattern and you begin to see a whale, an elephant, or a rocket ship. Another person may not be able to see what you see and for that person the clouds remain random and formless. You cannot argue another into seeing the whale or present evidence that any competent observer would have to agree makes it highly probable that it is a whale. You can only direct the other's attention to the clouds and hope that he or she will see them that way too.

The English philosopher John Wisdom has provided an interesting analogy that may help us to understand the matter.[9] He imagines two people returning to a long-neglected garden. Despite the weeds there are some plants still thriving. They inspect the garden together and note all the details. One of them thinks that perhaps a gardener has come to tend the place in their absence and sees in the arrangement of the plants a purpose and feel for beauty. No one, however, has seen a gardener come and there is no other evidence that a gardener has been coming. Despite the lack of evidence, one of them maintains that there is a gardener. Wisdom is explicit that the gardener hypothesis has become no longer empirical. The intriguing thing about this example is that, while both men are aware of all the facts about the garden and they both agree that there is no evidence that a gardener has been coming, they differ in their response to it. One sees in it a pattern that speaks of concern; the other finds it just weedy.

Wisdom's garden analogy will only take us so far, but it should suggest that part of being religious is seeing and reacting to the world in certain ways, thinking of it, for example, as being in the care of a "Master Gardener." The religious person, the Jew, the Christian, or the Muslim, must not only understand the world as God's world, but also come to see other people as children of God and thus like one's own brothers and sisters. And that, of course, must entail a way of living in the world, a way of relating to other people and of understanding oneself. Wisdom's garden does not entail that consequence. From this perspective we can also understand something about the position of the non-religious person. Non-believers need not *deny* anything; that is, they need not claim that statements of religious belief are false or that God does not exist. It is, rather, that they do not see things in that way. The facts of the world do not organize for them as they do for believers nor do they live in the world as believers do.

This latter point requires more explanation. Atheists are characterized by their denial that God exists; they take the proposition "God exists" to be false. We have said, however, that the non-believer does not necessarily have to play the role of atheist and deny the believer's position. We can understand this way of looking at the matter by reference to something that Ludwig Wittgenstein said.

There are religious people who think of things that happen in the world as rewards or punishments from God. Wittgenstein asks us to imagine someone who thinks of everything that happens to him as a reward or punishment and then to imagine another person who does not think of it that way at all. He says:

> Suppose someone is ill and he says: "This is a punishment," and I say: "If I'm ill, I don't think of punishment at all." If you say: "Do you believe the opposite?" – you can call it believing the opposite, but it is entirely different from what we would normally call believing the opposite.

> I think differently, in a different way. I say different things to myself. I have different pictures.
>
> It is this way: If someone said: "Wittgenstein, you don't take illness as punishment, so what do you believe?" – I'd say: "I don't have any thoughts of punishment."[10]

In his imagined role in this conversation Wittgenstein is not denying that illness is a punishment, that is, he is not claiming that the statement "This is a punishment" is false. The claim that it is false is the sort of thing that would be said by someone who shares the same *picture*, the same view of life and the world as the one who takes it to be punishment. From within that particular religious perspective there could be a dispute about whether this illness is or is not a punishment. One may understand it as God's retribution for something he had done while the other may say that what was done was not the sort of thing to merit God's retribution. Here it may be useful to recall the discussions between Job and his so-called "comforters." They try to convince Job that his misfortunes are the result of his sins while Job steadfastly maintains that he has never sinned, that is, transgressed the Mosaic law. Those who do not share a religious view of things, or that particular religious view, however, make no connection at all between illnesses and punishment; they don't think in that way.

If we put aside the question of whether God exists as somehow a mistaken or at least irrelevant question for the believer, then we can better understand the other "reasons" that people can give as reasons for "believing that God exists." For both the Jew and the Christian their religious faith and the Bible are very closely connected. It is surely a mistake to think of the Bible as a kind of reference book to which disputing parties can turn to settle the question of the existence of God as they might turn to the encyclopedia to settle their dispute about whether there really is a King of France. It is probably closer to the mark to say that for Jews and Christians religious faith and acceptance of the Bible go together; they are, we might say, bought as a package.[11] To believe in God is to be religious and part of being religious is to accept the Bible. From within the context of religious faith passages from the Bible can then be used to support this or that doctrine and to serve as ammunition in this or that doctrinal dispute. It cannot, of course, be used in any dispute with non-believers because an essential part of that kind of dispute concerns the place of the Bible itself.

Two of the other "reasons" for believing that God exists enter very naturally at this point. One person says he has been taught to believe and another remarks on how belief has changed her life. The majority of religious people have doubtless been taught their religion; they have grown up in a family where they were encouraged to attend divine services, to read the Bible, and to pray. If it is correct to think of religion as a way of life, then this is what we should expect. A way of life has to be passed on from one generation to another. Tradition is a very important element in the religious life and many people are sustained in their religious faith by the knowledge that they are participating in and continuing practices that were begun centuries in the past. In his *Letters from Prison* Dietrich Bonhoeffer wrote, "The consciousness of being borne up by a spiritual tradition that goes back for centuries gives one a feeling of confidence and security in the face of all passing strains and stresses."[12]

If we are to think of religion in terms of a way of living, then, of course, the life of the person raised in a religious atmosphere and taught to be religious will be different in certain respects from that of one who does not come from such a background. Especially interesting are cases of people who, not being religious, become religious or experience a religious conversion and thereby come to understand themselves and the world very differently from the way they did before.

It will be helpful here to look at one of the very first, and perhaps most notable, conversions, that of St Paul. Paul – Saul was his Hebrew name[13] – was a Jew who was opposed to the new sect of believers in Jesus within Judaism and undertook actively to work against them. On the road to Damascus he had some kind of transforming experience[14] and changed from being a persecutor of the sect to being the Apostle to the Gentiles. He was the single individual most responsible for the development of the new faith. Paul describes the change in his life this way.

> You have heard what my manner of life was when I was still a practicing Jew: how savagely I persecuted the church of God and tried to destroy it; and how in the practice of our national religion I outstripped most of my Jewish contemporaries by my boundless devotion to the traditions of my ancestors.
>
> But then in his good pleasure God, who from my birth had set me apart, and who had called me through his grace, chose to reveal his Son in and through me, in order that I might proclaim him to the Gentiles. (Galatians 1:13–16)

Paul's conversion, to be sure, was not from non-belief to belief, but from one religious position to another. The principle of a change of perspective, however, remains the same.

One of the most detailed and literary accounts of religious conversion is that by St Augustine in his *Con-*

fessions. In that book Augustine describes his early life and his eventual conversion to Christianity. Augustine's mother, St Monica, was a Christian, but his father was not and although he received some religious training as a youth it did not at the time influence his life. He was very well educated and became a respected teacher of rhetoric. All things considered, one would think him a fine chap. He was intelligent, loved his mother, was affable, and made friends easily. He was fond of what can be called the pleasures of the flesh and kept a mistress for many years, but was loyal to her and fond of the illegitimate son that she bore him. He was, nevertheless, spiritually troubled and sought solace in various systems of Greek philosophy that he studied thoroughly before he gave himself to Christianity.

A striking feature of Augustine's account of his life prior to his conversion is that he describes his actions in terms of *sin*. The word "sin," we must remind ourselves, is not just a synonym for "morally wrong," but carries the sense of being an offense against God. To describe what one does as a sin demands a religious perspective. It is only in the light of his conversion that he could understand his earlier life as sinful and his former ways as something to be avoided. He says, addressing God,

> The good which I now sought was not outside myself. I did not look for it in things which are seen with the eye of the flesh by the light of the sun. For those who try to find joy in things outside themselves easily vanish away into emptiness. They waste themselves on the temporal pleasures of the visible world. . . . But it was in my inmost heart, where I had grown angry with myself, where I had been stung with remorse, where I had slain my old self and offered it in sacrifice, where I had first purposed to renew my life and placed my hope in you, it was there that you

> had begun to make me love you and had *made me glad at heart.*[15]

The fact that religious belief can work changes in a person's life has an interesting logical status that in certain respects is shared by several of the other notions that we have been considering such as belief in the Bible and in miracles. That religion has changed a person's life cannot possibly count as evidence for the existence of God for the non-believer. For one thing, there are too many alternative explanations that cannot be summarily dismissed in favor of the untestable God hypothesis and, for another, lives can change, and change radically, for better or for worse, in circumstances where religion does not enter at all.[16] Religious believers will, of course, describe their own conversion and that of others as the result of God's activity as does Paul in the passage from Galatians quoted above. To describe it in that way, however, already presupposes a religious standpoint and cannot be the grounds for religious belief. To say that it is God that entered one's life must be understood as an expression of religious faith and not an explanation that just anyone, including non-believers, could agree to. There is an analogy here with those who believe in miracles and put their trust in the Bible. To speak of miracles and to rely upon the Bible, we have insisted, is already to be religious.

Father Sergius

Our suggestion that religious faith involves, among other things, a way of life is given a fascinating illustration in Leo Tolstoy's story *Father Sergius*. *Father Sergius* tells of a young man of the minor nobility who destined himself for a career in the army. He was highly intelligent, even brilliant, proud, and ambitious. He sought to excel in everything he did and, indeed, he did. He was devoted to the Tsar and aspired to become his military aide. In that way he could satisfy his ambition to be welcomed into the inner circles of the court. As a means to this latter end he began to pay court to a beautiful and charming young lady of the high nobility, but he also came to be very much in love with her. At first her response to him was cool but then she suddenly changed and gave him every encouragement. They were engaged to be married. Two weeks before the marriage was to take place she confessed to him that she had been for a while the Tsar's mistress. He immediately ended the engagement and as soon as it could be arranged he resigned from the army and entered a monastery, eventually taking the name Father Sergius. His mother tried to dissuade him from this step, but his sister understood what he was doing.

> She understood that he had become a monk in order to be above those who considered themselves his superiors. And she understood him correctly. By becoming a monk he showed contempt for all that seemed most important to others and that had seemed so to him while he was in the service, and he now ascended a height from which he could look down on those he had formerly envied.[17]

There was, nevertheless, in him a genuine religious sense that his sister was unaware of.

As a monk he desired to be the best of all possible monks just as he had desired to excel in everything else in life. He did try to control his pride and his fleshly appetites. This was not easy for him to do, especially when he was sought out by people who had known him in his other life and found him something of a celebrity. He eventually retired to a hermit's cell dug into the hillside at another monastery.

One night a beautiful and wealthy divorcee wagered with her friends that she could spend the night with Father Sergius whose past was well known to them. She attempted to seduce him and to control the passion that nearly mastered him he chopped off a finger with the wood-cutting axe. The woman was shocked by the consequence of what she had tried to do and shortly after the incident she withdrew from the world and entered a convent.

As the years passed Father Sergius achieved a reputation for curing the sick and pilgrims came from far and wide to visit and see the holy man. On one occasion a man brought his somewhat retarded daughter of 22 years to him in hopes that he could help her. The girl was left with him and proved more than willing to lead him into temptation. It was too much for Father Sergius and he was overcome by the flesh. The next morning, horrified by the situation, he cut his hair, put on peasant clothes, and slipped away from his cell, abandoning the occupation of hermit monk for ever.

He was in despair and considered suicide. He exclaimed that there was no God. "As usual at moments of despair he felt the need of prayer. But there was no one to pray to. There was no God."

He fell asleep and dreamed of a woman whom he had known when they were children. She had been an awkward, unattractive child whom the boys had made fun of. He awoke with a desire to see her once more and set out for where he knew she lived, a journey of some two hundred miles. She had married a drunkard who had left her with two children and nothing else. Her son had died and her daughter had married a worthless chap who could not work and now she was the sole support of the daughter, son-in-law and five grandchildren who all lived under her roof. She eked out a living by giving piano lessons to some village children.

Sergius spent the day at her house. She had at first taken him for a homeless beggar and was going to give him a small coin and a bit of bread. He confessed his sins to her and she told him that she no longer went to church, that she sometimes prayed, but only in a mechanical fashion. She believed that her present miserable life was God's punishment for her sins. Sergius reflected on his visit to her and said to himself that she

> ". . . is what I ought to have been but failed to be. I lived for men on the pretext of living for God, while she lives for God imagining that she lives for men. Yes, one good deed – a cup of water given without thought of reward – is worth more than any benefit I imagined I was bestowing on people. But after all was there not some share of sincere desire to serve God?" he asked himself, and the answer was: "Yes, there was, but it was all soiled and overgrown by desire for human praise. Yes, there is no God for the man who lives, as I did, for human praise. I will now seek Him!"

He became a wandering pilgrim begging meals and a place to sleep. Finally he was arrested as a vagrant and exiled to Siberia where "he has settled down as the hired man of a well-to-do peasant, in which capacity he works in the kitchen garden, teaches children, and attends to the sick."

The interesting philosophical aspect of the story emerges when we seek to understand Father Sergius' statement that there is no God. Are we to take him as expressing a proposition that denies the proposition expressed by Anselm, Aquinas, Cleanthes, and so many others that there is a God? Let's try to imagine one of those philosophers encountering Sergius shortly after he had left his cell and as he contemplated suicide. "So you say there is no God," we can imagine him saying to Sergius. "Well, I have a neat little argument here and, if you take the trouble to work through it, it will convince you otherwise. Refute it if you can." This picture is, of course, ludicrous. This is not the time for an intellectual debate. Father Sergius' "There is no God" is not offered as a *proposition* whose truth value is on the table for discussion; it is, rather, a cry of despair. He has at last realized that his pride and ambition were always stronger than his religious faith. When he said that "there is no God for the man who lives, as I did, for human praise" we do not have to understand him to be denying a proposition that others have affirmed. We can understand his expression, instead, as making the conceptual point that to live for human praise is not to live a truly religious life.

There can also be a certain amusement in the picture of the philosophers confronting Sergius after the resolution of his spiritual crisis and his exile to Siberia. They explain to him their arguments and then ask him whether, as a truly religious man, he does not agree with them. We can imagine him replying, "That's all very interesting and when I was a young student it surely would have intrigued me, but there are things to be done now. So won't you come with me to help teach the children and tend the sick?"

Tolstoy's story presents us with a picture of religion as a way of living, as a way of understanding oneself and one's relations with other people. It is worth noting that this story which is such a profound exploration of religious faith contains no reference to doctrine or any particular religious belief. Although Tolstoy never deals with the matter, it is not difficult for us to conclude from his story that reliance upon believing certain propositions to be true may simply not be relevant to Father Sergius' religious life. We may generalize from this that emphasis on holding propositions to be true is by no means a necessary part of religion and perhaps should not be the focus of attention in the philosophy of religion.

Philosophy and the Philosophy of Religion

When we first talked about the subject of the philosophy of religion in the Introduction we declined to offer definitions of either religion or philosophy. The conception of philosophy expressed in this book was said to be something that would emerge as we went along. It is now time to make explicit what it is that has emerged.

We have seen that one of the major tools in the philosopher's kit is logic and argumentation. Philosophers must be prepared to argue for their conclusions and to evaluate critically their own arguments as well as whatever arguments are presented to them. Arguments, however, are not the end of philosophy. Philosophers are not like debaters whose aim is to refute the arguments of their opponents so that their own will carry the day. Philosophy's aim is to get to a better understanding of things and wherever possible to arrive at the truth about them.

The things that philosophy seeks to understand are not, however, the things that science investigates; it is not the behavior of the observable phenomena of the world and how they are to be explained that concerns philosophy. Several times we have spoken of our questions as conceptual ones, questions about our ideas and concepts. Our concepts are embedded in and expressed by the words of our language. Philosophy as a conceptual investigation undertakes to map relations between our concepts and to determine what it makes sense to say and what it does not make sense to say.

In chapter 2, for example, we noted that the conclusion of the ontological argument that God is a necessary being could be understood as telling us something about the concept, the idea of God. It tells us that it makes no sense to ask the kind of questions about God that we ask about people, e.g. How old is He?, Where was He born? and the like. In this way we can see that there is no conceptual relation between the idea of God and the idea of having an age or a place of birth. On the positive side of the ledger, by contrast, we can note the important conceptual connections between God and creation, God and love, and so on. Of course, not everything that we can say about one person loving another applies to God. God does not send roses to a beloved nor ask for a hand in marriage. It is a good philosophical exercise to think of all the things it makes sense to say about a person who loves and then note how much or how little of that applies to God.

The point of mapping these conceptual relations is not simply to come up with a catalogue of all possible connections between our ideas, but to help us find our way through certain problems. One of these problems is the justification of religious beliefs: How can religious beliefs be shown to be true? A little reflection will remind us that this has been the topic of most of these chapters. Some have tried to do this through logical arguments, some by appealing to historical or scientific evidence, and then there are those anti-religious people who delight in pointing out that the arguments don't work and that the evidence doesn't exist. People caught in the middle of all this may feel thoroughly puzzled and all at sea.

One of the tentative conclusions of this book is that this whole controversy is misguided. It arises because of a failure to understand religious concepts. Religious statements are not like the propositions of mathematics or logic which can be established by deduction. Nor are they like those of science to be shown true by gathering evidence. "What evidence is there for the existence of God?" is not a proper question. The concept of God and the concept of evidence don't go together. Once these conceptual issues are understood we are able to understand our concerns and activities much more clearly. Religious believers can realize that they don't have to convert heathens or refute atheists with arguments and evidence, arguments that are invariably bad and evidence that is more than suspicious, but can get on with serving God, teaching the children, tending the sick, and being an example for those they seek to influence. And atheists, in their turn, can give up belittling believers for their intellectual naivety and be content with the realization that they do not see the world that way nor live that kind of life.

There is a question about all this that arises very naturally. Where do we get the appropriate information about these concepts and how do we determine what it does and does not make sense to say? To answer this very important question we must remind ourselves that, just as our concepts are embedded in our language, so our language is embedded in our life. Language cannot be understood apart from its setting in the context of our activities and practices. We see people sitting around a table and hear them saying in turn "One heart"; "Two diamonds"; "Pass." These expression get their sense from the role they play in the game of bridge. Think how differently the expression "two diamonds" functions in bridge from the way it does when the jeweler takes inventory in the shop or the difference in "one heart" in the game and "one heart" in the anatomy lab. The sense lies not in the sentence itself, but in its roles in human life.

One of the problems we face in doing philosophy is that expressions that really have very different uses and meanings can look quite alike when we fail to take into account the context of their use. "A miracle occurred" and "A volcanic eruption occurred" have exactly the same grammatical form and this can mislead us into supposing that we must look for the evidence of the miracle just as we look for the evidence of volcanic activity. Here we must keep in mind the very different role that religious statements play from statements made in the context of scientific investigation.

The fact that the same word or expression can play different roles in different circumstances opens wonderful opportunities for conceptual jokes. There is a Groucho Marx routine in which Stuffed Shirt emerges from the hotel and demands "Call me a taxi!" Groucho obliges by saying, "Okay, so you're a taxi." Alice tells Humpty Dumpty that her age is seven years and six months. Humpty tells her that is an awkward age and that she should have stopped at seven. Alice objects that "one can't help growing older," to which Humpty replies, "*One* can't, perhaps, but *two* can."[18]

We must look to the practice of religion itself for our understanding of talk of God, miracles, the Bible, and all the rest. This is why the philosophy of religion requires that we begin with at least some familiarity with religion. We do not have to be religious in order to be philosophers of religion, but we must have some acquaintance with what religious people say and do, how they pray and worship, and how they think of the world, themselves, and other people. We can note, for example, that from within the practice of religion believers do not ask for evidence to confirm their belief. Demanding evidence for one's views, by contrast, is an essential feature within the practice of science. Thus we can see clearly that religion and science are very different sorts of things and that it would be a mistake to insist that the one adopt the practice of the other or risk being labeled a failure. Note that it did not take any special expertise or access to privileged information to realize this; our common and very ordinary understanding of these aspects of life was quite enough.

And now a final word about religion. It is very probably a mistake to suppose that there is some essence of religion, some central core to be found in all religions of whatever age or place. Religions are many and varied and take many different forms. We have restricted ourselves to the monotheistic religions of Judaism and Christianity, but even there we find a host of variations and differences. A theme that unites both Judaism and Christianity is the belief in one God, but there are important differences in this belief. Judaism calls its faithful to "Hear O Israel! The Lord our God, the Lord is one" (Deuteronomy 6:4)[19] while Christianity insists upon its Trinitarian creed that God is Three yet somehow One. Even within each of these religions there are significant differences in how the various doctrines and creeds are understood. All Jews profess attachment to the Mosaic law, but which parts are to observed or ignored and how they are to be observed is a matter of disagreement. Christians have and still do hold widely varying views about the nature of Christ, the role of Mary and the Virgin Birth, and the importance of the sacraments, to name only a few.

We shall not try to define religion and, fortunately for our purposes, it is not necessary to do so. We can, however, point out some important features that are characteristic of both Judaism and Christianity as well as a number of other religions. Both insist upon certain beliefs and doctrines although Christianity puts much more emphasis on doctrine than does Judaism. Both make use of public worship and rituals as well as private prayer. Both place great reliance upon the traditions of the faith and the importance of connecting believers with a tradition of belief and worship. Both have a strong ethical content and seek to provide their adherents with a way to live their lives. These features, beliefs, ritual, prayer, tradition, and ethics are found in many variations. Some groups within the religions put greater emphasis on this or that one rather than on these others.

Itemizing the details of all that belongs to the historical and comparative study of religion and not to the philosophy of religion. Some awareness of these features is quite enough both to generate the problems of the philosophy of religion and to provide the resources for the kind of philosophical clarification we have been seeking. Whether or not any useful measure of that clarification has been achieved must be left to the reader to determine.

Suggestions for Further Reading

A good source for the understanding of logical positivism is A. J. Ayer, ed., *Logical Positivism* (Glencoe: The Free Press, 1959).

For reactions of Bultmann's views see Rudolph Bultmann, *Kerygma and Myth*, ed. Werner Bartsch (New York: Harper & Bros, 1961).

Other works that present accounts of religion similar to the one expressed here are Cyril Barrett, *Wittgenstein on Ethics and Religious Belief* (Oxford: Basil Blackwell, 1991); Fergus Kerr, *Theology After Wittgenstein* (Oxford: Basil Blackwell, 1986); Robert T. Herbert, *Paradox and Identity in Theology* (Ithaca and London: Cornell University Press, 1979); and several works of D. Z. Phillips, *The Concept of Prayer* (London: Routledge & Kegan Paul, 1965); *Belief, Change and Forms of Life* (Basingstoke: Macmillan, 1986); *Faith After Foundationalism* (London and New York: Routledge, 1988).

An interesting way of reading the Bible for its religious significance without falling into the inerrantist trap is shown in Harry A. Nielsen, *The Bible – as if for the First Time* (Philadelphia: Westminster Press, 1984).

For accounts of the conception of philosophy presented here see John Wilson, *Thinking With Concepts* (Cambridge: Cambridge University Press, 1966), and O. K. Bouwsma's essay, "The Blue Book", in O. K. Bouwsma, *Philosophical Essays* (Lincoln: University of Nebraska Press, 1965).

Notes

1. "Gnosis" is derived from a Greek word meaning knowledge. When the negative prefix is added the word means "no knowledge."
2 Ayer's criticism of religious statements is found in his book *Language, Truth and Logic*, 2nd edn (New York: Dover Publications, 1946), pp. 114ff. Ayer's book remains one of the best expositions of both the theories and the spirit of logical positivism.
3 We must be careful to avoid misunderstanding here. We read of a child in the old west who was captured by the

Indians and raised as one of them. At this distance there may be no way to confirm the story, all the participants are dead, the records have been destroyed and so on. We can nevertheless describe the kind of evidence that would be required to determine its truth although that evidence is no longer available. Pogo's description of his foster tribe as *invisible* Indians, by contrast, removes the very possibility that anything could ever count as evidence for its truth. Therein lies the beauty of his joke.

4 It is sometimes claimed that the church is founded upon the gospels, but this is not accurate as an historical claim. The church was not a product of the gospels, rather the gospels were a product of the early church. It also must be remembered that the fourth century creeds such as the Nicene Creed were formulated in terms of metaphysical concepts borrowed from Greek philosophy.

5 The following account of Bultmann's views is taken from his article "New Testament and Mythology," in *New Testament and Mythology*, ed. and trans. Schubert M. Ogden (Philadelphia: Fortress Press, 1984). The article was originally published in 1941.

6 "Eschatology" is a Greek word that refers to the last things, the end of the world, etc.

7 Bultmann, "New Testament and Mythology," p. 9.

8 Ibid, p. 41.

9 John Wisdom, "Gods," *Proceedings of the Aristotelian Society* (194445); repr. in Anthony Flew, ed., *Logic and Language*, first series (Oxford: Basil Blackwell, 1955). A criticism of Wisdom's article is presented by Anthony Flew's article, "Theology and Falsification," in Anthony Flew and Alasdair Macintyre, eds, *New Essays in Philosophical Theology* (New York: Macmillan, 1956).

10 Ludwig Wittgenstein, *Lectures & Conversations on Aesthetics, Psychology and Religious Belief*, ed. Cyril Barrett (Berkeley and Los Angeles: University of California Press, 1972), p. 55.

11 To say that Jews and Christians accept the Bible, read it, turn to it in times of tribulation, use it in religious services, and so on, does not entail any commitment to the doctrine of Biblical inerrancy. One must look to see how it is used, how it is read, what passages are selected for emphasis, what is ignored, and the like.

12 Dietrich Bonhoeffer, *Letters and Papers from Prison*, enlarged edition, ed. Eberhard Bethge (New York: Macmillan, 1971), p. 165.

13 The Hebrew name Saul transliterates into the Greek as a dirty word, hence the change to Paul.

14 The nature of this experience is not altogether clear. There are three accounts of it in Acts (chapters 9, 22, 26) which are by no means consistent.

15 St Augustine, *Confessions*, trans. R. S. Pine-Coffin, Book IX, §4. William James, in *The Varieties of Religious Experience* (New York: Longmans, Green & Co., 1902), describes a number of interesting examples of both religious and non-religious lives and views of life and how these can change as a result of conversion.

16 James, *Varieties of Religious Experience*, cites a number of these cases.

17 The translation is that of Louise and Aylmer Maude, in *Great Short Works of Tolstoy* (New York: Harper & Row, 1976).

18 Lewis Carroll's *Through the Looking Glass* is a marvelous budget of conceptual jokes and for that reason is a favorite of philosophers. It is a great help to students of philosophy to become attuned to the nuances of language and to acquire a nose for when words are being misused and language is going astray.

19 Jews call this statement "Shema" which is Hebrew for "hear," the first word of the passage. It is an essential part of Jewish liturgy. It has been interpreted as an explicit rejection of the Christian Trinitarian view of God.

Index